THE CHURCH AND THE KINGDOM

CHURCH THE BODY OF CHRIST

LESLIE M. JOHN

Leslie M. John

THE CHURCH AND THE KINGDOM

CHURCH THE BODY OF CHRIST

LESLIE M. JOHN

The entire text of this book and graphics are deposited with Library of Congress Copyright Office, 101 Independence Avenue, SE Washington, DC 20559-6000, USA. This work is protected by Law in US; and internationally, according to The Berne Convention 1971

ISBN-10:0989905810
ISBN-13:978-0-9899058-1-7

Contents

PREFACE

My mission is to proclaim the good news of our Lord Jesus Christ as revealed to me through Holy Bible and from various teachers, preachers, and commentators. This is my voluntary service to God in the name of His only begotten Son Lord Jesus Christ.

I share the truth of knowledge of God with others with good intention of bringing them to the knowledge of the living God, the God of Abraham, the God of Isaac, the God of Jacob, and the Father of our Lord Jesus Christ. My mission is to proclaim the Gospel of Lord Jesus Christ and not converting forcibly anyone to Christianity.

There are fundamental Christian doctrines that I believe in and I will not compromise on those doctrines. They are:

God is Triune: The Father, The Son and The Holy Spirit. They are not three Gods, but One God in three persons, co-equal-co-existent and functionally different.

There is no salvation except by Grace through Faith in Lord Jesus Christ. I believe in:

"That if thou shalt confess with thy mouth the Lord Jesus, and shalt believe in thine heart that God hath raised him from the dead, thou shalt be saved" (Romans 10:9)

One may accept or reject any or part of my writings/teachings. No offense is meant to any individual or any religion or any organization. Please visit http://www.lesliejohn.net/

I pray for the peace of Jerusalem and desire that all Jews may accept Lord Jesus as their personal Savior and Messiah.

"Pray for the peace of Jerusalem: they shall prosper that love thee" (Psalms 122:6)

I firmly believe in the saying of Jesus, who said:

"No man can come to me, except the Father which hath sent me draw him: and I will raise him up at the last day" John 6:44.

My efforts to teach or preach are of no use unless Lord Jesus Christ Himself intervenes and the Father draws a person unto Him.

All Scriptures in electronic format are from King James Version (KJV) from Open domain.

Description:

This book brings out the marvelous truth about the mystery that was hidden in the Old Testament period now made known by the revelation through Apostle Paul. The mystery is that Lord Jesus Christ is the head of the Church, upon Him is the Church built, and all the believers in Him, are the members of His body. Salvation is by Grace through Faith in Lord Jesus Christ.

"And to make all men see what is the fellowship of the mystery, which from the beginning of the world hath been hid in God, who created all things by Jesus Christ" (Ephesians 3:9)

"That the Gentiles should be fellowheirs, and of the same body, and partakers of his promise in Christ by the gospel" (Ephesians 3:6)

"That if thou shalt confess with thy mouth the Lord Jesus, and shalt believe in thine heart that God hath raised him from the dead, thou shalt be saved" (Romans 10:9)

"I and my Father are one" (John 10:30)

CHAPTER 1
THE BODY OF CHRIST

We would know the true meaning of the Church if we could appreciate the words of Adam when he saw the woman. The LORD God caused a deep sleep to fall upon Adam and when he was sleeping God took one of his ribs and closed up the flesh in its place. God made the rib of man a woman and brought the woman unto man.

"And Adam said, This is now bone of my bones, and flesh of my flesh: she shall be called Woman, because she was taken out of Man". (Genesis 2:23)

The word of God says:

"Therefore shall a man leave his father and his mother, and shall cleave unto his wife: and they shall be one flesh". (Genesis 2:24)

This glorious truth is presented to us by Apostle Paul in Ephesians 5:22-25

"Wives, submit yourselves unto your own husbands, as unto the Lord. For the husband is the head of the wife, even as Christ is the head of the church: and he is the saviour of the body. Therefore as the church is subject unto Christ, so let the wives be to their own husbands in every thing. Husbands, love your wives, even as Christ also loved the church, and gave himself for it" (Ephesians 5:22-25)

The relationship between the husband and the wife is that husband is the head of the wife, even as Christ is the head of the Church. Christ is the savior of the body and he presents to himself a bride that is holy and without blemish.

"That he might present it to himself a glorious church, not having spot, or wrinkle, or any such thing; but that it should be holy and without blemish". (Ephesians 5:27)

All those whose sin is cleansed by the blood of Christ are the members of the Church, which is the body of Christ.

"Now ye are the body of Christ, and members in particular". (1 Corinthians 12:27)

The body of Christ is one and has many members who are the members of that one body, and being many members they are all one body.

The body of Christ is baptized by one Spirit irrespective of whether we are Jews or Gentiles, or bond or free. One part of the body cannot say to the other that it has no need of the other. Foot cannot call itself separate from the body because it is not hand, nor can eye can call itself separate because it is not ear, nor can anybody part say to the other that it has no need of the other part (1 Corinthians 12:12-24). The whole body suffers if one of its members suffers loss or damage.

Church is not a building or simply a called out people, or congregation, or gathering of citizens, or social gathering, or discussion or debating forum. It is not also the "kingdom of heaven" or "kingdom of God". The Church is the "Body of Christ".

The Church is the "Bride of Christ". Careful observation of Ephesians Chapter 5 gives us the answer that the one who is presenting to Himself is Lord Jesus Christ and He is presenting to Himself a glorious Church that has no spot, or wrinkle of any such thing. Jesus is expecting from the Church that it should be without blemish.

What is the purpose of Jesus presenting to himself Church without blemish? It is because the Church is His bride, His own possession which was bought with a price and that price was His own blood shed on the cross. Christ is the head of the Church and He is the savior of the body.

The Church is subject unto Jesus Christ, who loved it so much so that he says a husband should love his wife just as He loved the Church. (Ephesians 5:23-25)

We also derive knowledge about "Church" from referring to Lexicon Hebrew Strong's Number 6951 and Greek Strong's Number 1577.

Hebrew Strong's Number: 6951 is "lhq" transliterated as "Qahal" pronounced as " kaw-hawl'" Its definition is: assembly, company, congregation, convocation, assembly for evil counsel, war or invasion, religious purposes, company (of returning exiles), congregation as organized body. The word occurs in the Old Testament 123 times in KJV – 17 times as "assembly" 17 times as "company" 86 times as "congregation" and 3 times as "multitude".

Greek Strong's Number: 1577 is: "eĺkklhsiða" transliterated as: "Ekklesia" pronounced as "ek-klay-see'-ah". Its definition is: "gathering of citizens called out from their homes into some public place", or "an assembly" or "an assembly of the people convened at the public place of the council for the purpose of deliberating" It could be "the assembly of the Israelites", "any gathering or throng of men assembled by chance, tumultuously" and in Christian sense "an assembly of Christians gathered for worship in a religious meeting". The word occurs in New Testament 118 times in KJV; 3 times as "Assembly" and 115 times as "Church".

The following few verses also help us to understand the meaning of the Church.

"And I say also unto thee, That thou art Peter, and upon this rock I will build my church; and the gates of hell shall not prevail against it." (Matthew 16:18)

"Praising God, and having favour with all the people. And the Lord added to the church daily such as should be saved". (Acts 2:47)

At the coasts of Caesarea Philippi Jesus asked his disciples as to what men say that He was? The disciples said some say that Jesus was John the Baptist, and some say that He was Prophet Elijah, and others Prophet Jeremiah or one of the prophets. But then, Jesus emphatically asked his disciples as to what they say of him.

Simon Peter, quick as he was always, said that Jesus was the Christ that is He was the Messiah, and the Jesus was the Son of the living God. What a great testimony Peter gave of Jesus! Then Jesus blessed Peter and said that flesh and blood did not reveal that fact to him but the Father in heaven.

. Holy Spirit came upon all those who were waiting at Jerusalem as instructed by Lord Jesus Christ and they were all filled with Holy Spirit and began to speak with other tongues as the Spirit gave them utterance. There were Jews, devout men, out of every nation under heaven at Jerusalem on that day (Acts 2:4, 5).

Some mocked saying that they were drunk, but Peter said that they were not drunk but that was what was spoken of prophet Joel spoke that God will pour out His "Spirit upon all flesh: and your sons and your daughters shall prophesy, and your young men shall see visions, and your old men shall dream dreams" (Acts 2:16-17, Joel 2:28).

Peter was the first disciple who spoke of Lord Jesus Christ's death on the cross, his burial and resurrection. Many from the audience received the word and "Then they that gladly received his word were baptized: and the same day there were added unto them about three thousand souls" (Acts 2:41).

As we read Acts Chapter 2 further we see that the Lord added to the church daily such as should be saved. It is clear here that the Church came into existence on Pentecost day as we read in Acts Chapter 2 and three thousand souls were added to the church and then the Lord added to the Church daily such as should be saved. (Acts 2:47)

Acts Chapter 11:1 says that apostles and brethren who were in Judea heard that Gentiles had also received the word of God.

When Peter went to Jerusalem they questioned him as to why he ate with those who were un-circumcised. Peter told them entire happening about how Cornelius, an un-circumcised Gentile was saved and how God told them not to treat anything as unclean (Acts Chapters 9 and 10).

This record shows that Gentiles were added to the Church. Neither Bible nor secular history says that all those who are from the regions mentioned in Acts 2 were pure descendants of Jacob.

The commission, indeed, was first to preach in Jerusalem, then in Judea and Samaria, and then to the uttermost part of the earth; but we see here that Gentiles heard the Gospel and were saved. They became part of the Church. They were called "Christians" first at Antioch.

Saul was converted and was named Paul and then in due course of time Barnabas departed to Tarsus to seek Saul. When he found him he brought him to Antioch and they assembled with the church and taught much people. They were then called "Christians" first at Antioch.

"Then departed Barnabas to Tarsus, for to seek Saul: And when he had found him, he brought him unto Antioch. And it came to pass, that a whole year they assembled themselves with the church, and taught much people. And the disciples were called Christians first in Antioch". (Acts 11:25-26)

The Church/Ecclesia that Lord Jesus Christ intended it to be like is not

1. A gathering of citizens called out from their homes into some public place, or

2. The whole body of nominal Christians scattered throughout the earth etc.

There is a tendency to link of the word Hebrew Word "qahal" of the Old Testament with the Greek word "ecclesia" in the New Testament based on the relationship that is present in Hebrews 2:12 with that of Psalm 22:22 and Matthew 26:30 and interpret that the Church was already begun in Matthew 26:30 with Jesus singing song along with his disciples after the Lord's Supper was instituted by Jesus Christ.

While this relationship is true and also that Jesus and disciples sang a song after the Passover is true these were only the basic elements shown in the case of Church/ecclesia. God never intended to build Church/ecclesia with only Jews and/or his disciples. That is not the right way of dividing the Scriptures.

"Study to shew thyself approved unto God, a workman that needeth not to be ashamed, rightly dividing the word of truth" (2 Timothy 2:15)

"And I say also unto thee, That thou art Peter, and upon this rock I will build my church; and the gates of hell shall not prevail against it". (Matthew 16:18)

The crucifixion of Jesus was yet to come when he instituted the Lord's Supper. Secondly, Matthew 28:18-19 Commission did not come into effect until after Pentecost was fully come and Holy Spirit came upon all those who were waiting at Jerusalem as per the instruction of Jesus. The commission came into effect only after Acts 1:8

"But ye shall receive power, after that the Holy Ghost is come upon you: and ye shall be witnesses unto me both in Jerusalem, and in all Judaea, and in Samaria, and unto the uttermost part of the earth" (Acts 1:8)

"And there were dwelling at Jerusalem Jews, devout men, out of every nation under heaven. Now when this was noised abroad, the multitude came together, and were confounded, because that every man heard them speak in his own language. And they were all amazed and marvelled, saying one to another, Behold, are not all these which speak Galilaeans? And how hear we every man in our own tongue, wherein we were born? Parthians, and Medes, and Elamites, and the dwellers in Mesopotamia, and in Judaea, and Cappadocia, in Pontus, and Asia, Phrygia, and Pamphylia, in Egypt, and in the parts of Libya about Cyrene, and strangers of Rome, Jews and proselytes, Cretes and Arabians, we do hear them speak in our tongues the wonderful works of God". (Acts 2:5-11)

There is a long list of countries, cities, towns mentioned in Acts 2:5-11. There is considerable disagreement about the people from these regions who were at Jerusalem during Passover festival, Unleavened bread and First-fruits, and Pentecost. The disagreement is as to whether they were Jews only or Jews and others.

Except for feast of Pentecost all other feasts had just been over at the time when Jesus gave instructions to his disciples to wait at Jerusalem until they receive power from heaven to go to nations to proclaim the Gospel of Jesus Christ.

Apostles had not yet preached the Gospel of Jesus Christ until then. Prior to ascension of Jesus Christ into heaven all that they knew was about probable restoration of the kingdom.

They asked Jesus when He would restore the kingdom; but He gave them reply that it was not for them to know the time that was in the authority of His Father (Acts 1:7). That was a feast time and when people gathered at Jerusalem to celebrate the festival and many others, who were, perhaps at there to do business.

There is no indication that all that were at Jerusalem at that time were Jews only. It reads "Jews, devout men, out of every nation under heaven".

If only Jews were there then other names would not have been there, but presence of other names and other regions confirms that the people there were not only Jews but Gentiles also. Scriptures and secular history do not say that "Parthians", "Medes", and "Elamites" were Jews. Genesis Chapter 10 and genuine historical record of Flavius Joseph proves that those present at Jerusalem during the feast of Pentecost were descendants of Jacob and also Gentiles.

Peter spoke and testified the death, burial and resurrection of Jesus Christ. Acts 2:14-33.

This is the first ever proclamation of the death of Jesus, his burial and resurrection was made and it was done by the one whom Jesus spoke of earlier. When Peter spoke of Jesus Christ there were three thousands souls added to them. It is very apt to note here that the audience present when Peter spoke about Jesus Christ was not only Jews but many others. Peter addressed them as "Men and brethren".

"Men and brethren, this scripture must needs have been fulfilled, which the Holy Ghost by the mouth of David spake before concerning Judas, which was guide to them that took Jesus" (Acts 1:16)

It should be noted that there were not only Jews but many others were present at the time when Peter spoke. It cannot be said that they were all the direct descendants of Jacob to believe that only Jews were there at that time. This alleviates the thought that there were no Gentiles when Peter spoke. Surely there were Gentiles.

This is the first time Peter spoke about the Jesus Christ's death, burial and resurrection and this is the first time that there were three thousand souls were added to them.

According to the commission given by Lord Jesus Christ the disciples were asked to be his witnesses first in Jerusalem, and in all Judea and in Samaria, and then in the uttermost part of the earth (Acts 1:8).

Basically it means that the message of salvation should have been spoken to first to Jews, then to descendants of Jews who mixed with Gentiles, and then lastly to the

Gentiles. Peter and other disciples surely followed just as Lord Jesus Christ commanded. However, it is too much to presume that there were no Gentiles in Jerusalem when Peter was speaking to Jews.

If only Jews were present and none else, then it would also mean that only Jews crucified Jesus and no Gentile was responsible for crucifixion of Jesus. Obviously it means Gentiles would never be partakers of the death, burial and resurrection of Jesus. This is not the case. Those, who crucified Jesus, were representatives of you and me. It is our sin that crucified Jesus. It is because of all of us that Jesus died on the cross taking on himself our sin to redeem us from the bondage of sin.

"For he hath made him to be sin for us, who knew no sin; that we might be made the righteousness of God in him" (2 Corinthians 5:21)

It is hard to find evidence in the Scriptures or in the secular history if the people in the regions mentioned in Acts 2:9-10 or in 1 Peter 1:1 are the descendants of Jacob. If no evidence can be produced then there is no meaning in saying that a distinct dispensation started after Acts Chapter 28 as "One New Man".

The Church consists of Jews and Gentiles and the Church came into existence as recorded in Acts Chapter 2. All those who are saved by grace through faith in Jesus are the members of the Church and the Church is the "Body of Christ"

Jesus is the head of the Church. The Church is bought with the price and that price is the blood of Lord Jesus. No doubt, Jews were there at the time of crucifixion of

Jesus and also on the day of Pentecost, but it is too much to say that there were ONLY JEWS! Scriptures should speak of Scriptures and confirm them and not mere assumptions.

How sure is anyone to say that none of the Gentiles, not even Roman Soldiers, or Government Officials, were saved when Peter preached about Jesus in Acts 2? It is mere speculation that only Jews were saved when Peter preached?

The Church grew and the Lord added to the Church souls daily as such as should be saved (Acts 2:47). The Scriptures call this collection of believers who are the members of His body and worship him as the "Church".

Furthermore the members of this Church, who taught the word of God to much people became the disciples of Jesus and these disciples were called first in Antioch (Acts 11:26).

The commission of Jesus was to teach and make disciples of all nations, baptizing them in the name of the Father, and of the Son, and of the Holy Spirit. (Matthew 28:18-20)

Peter surely was addressing Jews in Acts 3:25-26 that they are the children of prophets, and of the covenant and that their fathers were Abraham, Isaac, and Jacob, unto whose children were the foremost privileges given of turning away from their iniquities and repent believing that God raised up his Son Jesus from the dead. They were surely blessed ones.

It is by grace by faith in Jesus that we are all saved. The children of Jacob refused to accept Jesus as their Messiah and then the disciples turned to Gentiles. There is not much record of his disciples preaching to the Gentiles. God kept their itineraries and preaching and where the lost ten tribes were as mystery to us. However, Paul's itineraries are recorded. Paul also preached first to Jews and then turned to Gentiles.

In Acts 13:46-47 we see that Paul and Barnabas became bold and said that it was necessary for them that the word of God should have been preached to Jews first. When they rejected their preaching they turned to Gentiles. Paul claims that he was chosen to be the light of the Gentiles and that he should speak of salvation unto the ends of the earth. (Acts 13:46-47)

The Lord spoke to Ananias about Paul that he was chosen vessel unto Him to bear His name before the Gentiles, and kings and the children of Israel.

"But the Lord said unto him, Go thy way: for he is a chosen vessel unto me, to bear my name before the Gentiles, and kings, and the children of Israel": (Acts 9:15)

Later on Paul became a very strong witness of Lord Jesus Christ and in spite of facing many trials and tribulations even imprisonment he did not give up preaching the Gospel of Jesus Christ. Paul said he was not ashamed of the gospel of Christ, because it was the power of God unto salvation first to Jew and then to Gentiles.

"For I am not ashamed of the gospel of Christ: for it is the power of God unto salvation to everyone that believeth; to the Jew first, and also to the Greek". (Romans 1:16)

For some people these verses may appear to be unimportant, but these verses surely help to form a solid ground for preaching Gospel (Cf. Acts Chapter 2:9-11 – They were all not Jews!)

I Chronicles Chapter 1:

Vs. 17 The sons of Shem; Elam, and Asshur, and Arphaxad, and Lud, and Aram, and Uz, and Hul, and Gether, and Meshech.

Vs. 18 And Arphaxad begat Shelah, and Shelah begat Eber.

Vs. 19 And unto Eber were born two sons: the name of the one was Peleg; because in his days the earth was divided: and his brother's name was Joktan.

Vs. 20 And Joktan begat Almodad, and Sheleph, and Hazarmaveth, and Jerah,

Vs. 21 Hadoram also, and Uzal, and Diklah,

Vs. 22 And Ebal, and Abimael, and Sheba,

Vs. 23 And Ophir, and Havilah, and Jobab. All these were the sons of Joktan. Vs. 24 Shem, Arphaxad, Shelah,

Vs. 25 Eber, Peleg, Reu,

Vs. 26 Serug, Nahor, Terah,

Vs. 27 Abram; the same is Abraham.

Vs. 28 The sons of Abraham; Isaac, and Ishmael.

Josephus, the noted historian says:

"the sons of Japhet; from Madai came the Madeans, who are called Medes, by the Greeks;"

"So did Riphath found the Ripheans, now called Paphlagonians; and Thrugramma the Thrugrammeans, who, as the Greeks resolved, were named Phrygians"

... and yet some Christians say that the three thousand souls saved (Acts 2:41) were all Jews!

The following is an excerpt from Flavius Joseph's record:

Quote: 4. Shem, the third son of Noah, had five sons, who inhabited the land that began at Euphrates, and reached to the Indian Ocean. For Elam left behind him the Elamites, the ancestors of the Persians. Ashur lived at the city Nineve; and named his subjects Assyrians, who became the most fortunate nation, beyond others. Arphaxad named the Arphaxadites, who are now called Chaldeans. Aram had the Aramites, which the Greeks called Syrians; as Laud founded the Laudites, which are now called Lydians. Of the four sons of Aram, Uz founded Trachonitis and Damascus: this country lies between Palestine and Celesyria. Ul founded Armenia; and Gather the Bactrians; and Mesa the Mesaneans; it is now called Charax Spasini. Sala was the son of Arphaxad; and his son was Heber, from whom they originally called the Jews Hebrews. Heber begat Joetan and Phaleg: he was called Phaleg, because he was born at the dispersion of the nations to their several countries; for Phaleg among the Hebrews signifies division. Now Joctan, one of the sons of Heber, had these sons, Elmodad, Saleph, Asermoth, Jera, Adoram, Aizel, Decla, Ebal, Abimael, Sabeus, Ophir, Euilat, and

Jobab. These inhabited from Cophen, an Indian river, and in part of Asia adjoining to it. And this shall suffice concerning the sons of Shem.

5. I will now treat of the Hebrews. The son of Phaleg, whose father was Heber, was Ragau; whose son was Serug, to whom was born Nahor; his son was Terah, who was the father of Abraham, who accordingly was the tenth from Noah, and was born in the two hundred and ninety-second year after the deluge; for Terah begat Abram in his seventieth year. Nahor begat Haran when he was one hundred and twenty years old; Nahor was born to Serug in his hundred and thirty-second year; Ragau had Serug at one hundred and thirty; at the same age also Phaleg had Ragau; Heber begat Phaleg in his hundred and thirty-fourth year; he himself being begotten by Sala when he was a hundred and thirty years old, whom Arphaxad had for his son at the hundred and thirty-fifth year of his age. Arphaxad was the son of Shem, and born twelve years after the deluge. Now Abram had two brethren, Nahor and Haran: of these Haran left a son, Lot; as also Sarai and Milcha his daughters; and died among the Chaldeans, in a city of the Chaldeans, called Ur; and his monument is shown to this day. These married their nieces. Nabor married Milcha, and Abram married Sarai. Now Terah hating Chaldea, on account of his mourning for Ilaran, they all removed to Haran of Mesopotamia, where Terah died, and was buried, when he had lived to be two hundred and five years old; Unquote

CHAPTER 2
THE BIRTH OF THE CHURCH

In Acts 1:4 we read that the disciples of Jesus were commanded not to depart from Jerusalem but wait for the Promise of the Father (Luke 24:49)

"And, being assembled together with [them], commanded them that they should not depart from Jerusalem, but wait for the promise of the Father, which, [saith he], ye have heard of me"

"And suddenly there came a sound from heaven as of a rushing mighty wind, and it filled all the house where they were sitting. And there appeared unto them cloven tongues like as of fire, and it sat upon each of them". (Acts 2:2-3)

After the ascension of Jesus they returned unto Jerusalem and they went up into upper room and they all continued in prayer with one accord. As we see in Acts Chapter 1:13 the disciples of Jesus, with the women, and Mary the mother of Jesus and with his brethren were in upper room and continued with one accord in prayer and supplication.

Acts 1:13 "And when they were come in, they went up into an upper room, where abode both Peter, and James, and John, and Andrew, Philip, and Thomas, Bartholomew, and Matthew, James [the son] of Alphaeus, and Simon Zelotes, and Judas [the brother] of James."

The narration continues to verse 15 and it says that in those days Peter stood up in the midst of all of them who were one hundred and twenty in number and spoke to them.

In Acts Chapter 2 we see that the day of Pentecost had finally come and they were all with one accord in one place. The sequence of the important three feasts was the Passover, the first-fruits and the Pentecost. Detailed description of all the feasts is listed in Leviticus Chapter 23. On the day of Passover Jesus was crucified; on the day of first-fruits Jesus rose from the dead and on the day of Pentecost the Church was born.

Jesus is called the first-fruits as we read in 1 Corinthians 15:23 "But every man in his own order: Christ the first-fruits; afterward they that are Christ's at his coming".

After Jesus rose from the dead he asked his disciples to wait at Jerusalem to receive the power. Jesus said to them they will be his witnesses after they receive the promise of the Father and that power was the Holy Spirit.

The promise of the Father that is the Holy Spirit came upon all the one hundred and twenty people including the disciples of Jesus and the mother of Jesus.

It was fiftieth day after the Passover feast. It was on Pentecost when the Holy Spirit came from heaven upon all those who were in upper room where the Church came into existence.

We are not asked to wait to receive the Holy Spirit, but He takes residence in every believer at the time of accepting Jesus as Savior.

There came from heaven, not from anywhere else, a sound from heaven as of a rushing mighty wind. The sound was from heaven and it was like a rushing mighty wind. It was not wind but it was like a rushing wind and when that sound came from heaven it filled the entire house where they were sitting.

Then there appeared unto them cloven tongues like of fire, not fire, but it was like fire and it sat upon each of them. There was no exclusion, but all of them had the cloven tongues like fire, not exactly fire, upon them. "Cloven" is past participle of "cleave".

That means everyone in the upper room saw the split or divided tongues like that of fire that came upon and sitting upon each of them.

When they were waiting in the upper room as Jesus commanded them to do, suddenly there came a sound from heaven like that of a rushing mighty wind, and it filled the entire house where they were sitting. Then there appeared to them split tongues like as of fire, not exactly fire, and it sat upon each one of them.

The promise of the Father was that they will not be left like orphans but the Comforter that is The Holy Spirit will be with them always. When they received the Holy Spirit they began to speak with other tongues as the Spirit gave them utterance.

They spoke in other tongues as the Spirit gave them utterance. They spoke different languages. Their speaking was not the utterance from the choices that the individuals could make, but it was as the Spirit gave them the utterance.

John said: "John answered them, saying, I baptize with water: but there standeth one among you, whom ye know not". John 1:26

Mar 1:8 I indeed have baptized you with water: but he shall baptize you with the Holy Ghost.

In Acts Chapter 2 what we see is that disciples were gathered in obedience to the commandment of Jesus. The occasion was the day of the birth of the Church; that is fiftieth day after the Passover feast and it was during the feast days in Jerusalem.

The utterances were the languages of the earth which every one of them understood. It was the time of three important feasts. Firstly, it was of Passover, secondly it was of first-fruits, and thirdly it was of Pentecost.

There were Jews, devout men, out of every nation under heaven in Jerusalem. When they all in Jerusalem heard the sound of the noise that came down from heaven like that of a mighty wind they were all surprised. There was no mighty wind but they heard the sound of the mighty wind that came down from heaven.

There was multitude of people in Jerusalem. There were Parthians, and Medes, and Elamites, and the dwellers in Mesopotamia, and in Judaea, and Cappadocia, in Pontus, and Asia, Phrygia, and Pamphylia, in Egypt, and in the parts of Libya about Cyrene, and strangers of Rome, Jews and proselytes, Cretes and Arabians.

The text in Acts 2:5-13 does not show that these all men were circumcised Proselytes. They all understood the languages that they spoke to one another and they marveled to see the signs and wonders of God.

They were all amazed and some mocked saying that they were drunk, but Peter lifted up his voice and said to them that they were not drunk. Peter said that as spoken by the Prophet Joel they all spoke in languages which were understood by all of them. (Acts 2:1-20)

CHAPTER 3
PETROS AND PETRA

"And I say also unto thee, That thou art Peter, and upon this rock I will build my church; and the gates of hell shall not prevail against it". (Matthew 16:18)

"Petra" and "Petros" are not English words; they are Greek words. There is something very important that needs our attention. Matthew 16:18 has brought-in much controversy as to what exactly this verse means. The question usually arises is as to whether Lord Jesus was saying to Peter that He would build His church upon Peter, or was He pointing to Himself and saying that He would build His church upon Himself.

Whenever there is a dispute about a word in the Bible it is essential that we refer to the original language from which they were translated.

Greek Strong's Number G4074 is "Petros" is translated as Peter or stone. The word occurs 161 times in Authorized Version (KJV).

Greek Strong's Number G4073 "Petra" is translated as "Rock". The word occurs 16 times in Authorized Version (KJV)

"And I say also unto thee, That thou art Peter (Petros), and upon this rock (Petra) I will build my church; and the gates of hell shall not prevail against it" (Matthew 16:18)

The verse by itself stripped from the context would give us a thought that Jesus was acknowledging Peter's affirmation that Jesus was the Son of God, and therefore, Jesus blessed him saying that Peter was the rock upon whom Jesus was going to build His church. The narration and the structure of the verse would substantiate this thought that Jesus was not intending to downplay the role of Peter, but blessed Him threefold, in approbation of his acknowledgment of the Lord as the Son of God.

However, if we view in larger sense, not only within the immediate context of the passage, but also in the context of the New Testament Truth as a whole, it is much more believable that Lord Jesus was saying that He was the head of the Church, and upon Him the Church would be built. The Church will have sustenance in Him, and the gates of hell shall not prevail against the Church. The second view is more acceptable than the view that the Church would be built upon Peter.

Peter was surely very much loved disciple of Jesus Christ and he was the one, who first admitted that Jesus Christ was the Son of the living God. Peter was surely senior among all the twelve disciples but He was not superior to any of the other disciples the Lord has chosen. Peter was an apostle but not a prince, either.

Lord Jesus Christ was so much pleased with Peter's reply that the Lord approved his acknowledgement and blessed him saying:

"...Blessed art thou, Simon Barjona: for flesh and blood hath not revealed it unto thee, but my Father which is in heaven. And I say also unto thee, That thou art Peter, and upon this rock I will build my church; and the gates of hell shall not prevail against it. And I will give unto thee the keys of the kingdom of heaven: and whatsoever thou shalt bind on earth shall be bound in heaven: and whatsoever thou shalt loose on earth shall be loosed in heaven. Then charged he his disciples that they should tell no man that he was Jesus the Christ" (Matthew 16:17-30)

Earlier, Peter said: "... Thou art the Christ, the Son of the living God" (Matthew 16:16)

There are three blessings embedded in one utterance from the Lord:

1.   That thou art Peter, and upon this rock I will build my church

2.   and the gates of hell shall not prevail against it,

3.   and I will give unto thee the keys of the kingdom of heaven: and whatsoever thou shalt bind on, earth shall be bound in heaven, and whatsoever thou shalt loose on earth shall be loosed in heaven.

The power of the word of Lord Jesus Christ was seen in healing the sick, calming the storm, feeding five thousand men with five fishes and two loaves. His was the creator and His word brought everything into existence.

Here, the Lord bestows exceedingly great blessings on Peter. The Lord said flesh and blood did not reveal to him that Jesus was the Son of God, but the Father in heaven revealed it to Him. The Lord was, in all probability was pointing to Himself, and said to Peter that He will build the Church upon Himself.

No satanic power will be able to stand against the Church. No evil attacks against it will prevail. Rightly so, Peter was the first one to proclaim the Gospel of Jesus Christ on the day of Pentecost. Acts Chapter 2 records the fruit of Peter's preaching.

"Then Peter said unto them, Repent, and be baptized every one of you in the name of Jesus Christ for the remission of sins, and ye shall receive the gift of the Holy Ghost. For the promise is unto you, and to your children, and to all that are afar off, even as many as the Lord our God shall call" (Acts 2:38-39)

"Then they that gladly received his word were baptized: and the same day there were added unto them about three thousand souls" (Acts 2:41)

"And they, continuing daily with one accord in the temple, and breaking bread from house to house, did eat their meat with gladness and singleness of heart, Praising God, and having favour with all the people. And the Lord added to the church daily such as should be saved" (Acts 2:46-47)

Peter was the first one to proclaim the Gospel to Jews, and then much later, he was the first apostle to proclaim the Gospel to Cornelius, a Gentile, as recorded in Acts Chapter 10:33-44

The foundation for the Church was laid on the apostles and prophets and thereafter, upon it, the Church was built with Jesus Christ Himself being the Chief

Cornerstone. Peter acknowledges that we are all living stones, and the head corner stone is Jesus. (Cf. 1 Peter 2:4-7)

"To whom coming, as unto a living stone, disallowed indeed of men, but chosen of God, and precious, Ye also, as lively stones, are built up a spiritual house, an holy priesthood, to offer up spiritual sacrifices, acceptable to God by Jesus Christ. Wherefore also it is contained in the scripture, Behold, I lay in Sion a chief corner stone, elect, precious: and he that believeth on him shall not be confounded. Unto you therefore which believe he is precious: but unto them which be disobedient, the stone which the builders disallowed, the same is made the head of the corner" (1 Peter 2:4-7)

Apostle Paul writes

"And are built upon the foundation of the apostles and prophets, Jesus Christ himself being the chief corner stone" (Ephesians 2:20)

Later, as we read in in 1 Corinthians 12th Chapter, Apostle Paul writes that Jesus is the head of the Church and all those who believe in Him are the members of that Church.

"For as the body is one, and hath many members, and all the members of that one body, being many, are one body: so also is Christ" (1 Corinthians 12:12)

"Now ye are the body of Christ, and members in particular. And God hath set some in the church, first apostles, secondarily prophets, thirdly teachers, after that miracles, then gifts of healings, helps, governments, diversities of tongues" (1 Corinthians 12:27-28)

Additional references:

The builder and the maker of the Church is Lord Jesus Christ.

"For other foundation can no man lay than that is laid, which is Jesus Christ" (1 Corinthians 3:11)

"And the Lord said, Who then is that faithful and wise steward, whom his lord shall make ruler over his household, to give them their portion of meat in due season?" (Luke 12:42

"Then take silver and gold, and make crowns, and set them upon the head of Joshua the son of Josedech, the high priest; And speak unto him, saying, Thus speaketh the LORD of hosts, saying, Behold the man whose name is The BRANCH; and he shall grow up out of his place, and he shall build the temple of the LORD: Even he shall build the temple of the LORD; and he shall bear the glory, and shall sit and rule upon his throne; and he shall be a priest upon his throne: and the counsel of peace shall be between them both" (Zechariah 6:11-13)

"That saith of Cyrus, [He is] my shepherd, and shall perform all my pleasure: even saying to Jerusalem , Thou shalt be built; and to the temple, Thy foundation shall be laid" Isaiah 44:28.

"Therefore thus saith the Lord GOD, Behold, I lay in Zion for a foundation a stone, a tried stone, a precious corner stone, a sure foundation: he that believeth shall not make haste" (Isaiah 28:16)

"Jesus answered and said unto them, Destroy this temple, and in three days I will raise it up. Then said the Jews, Forty and six years was this temple in building, and wilt thou rear it up in three days? But he spake of the temple of his body" John 2:19-21)

"And the wall of the city had twelve foundations, and in them the names of the twelve apostles of the Lamb". (Revelation 21:14)

Indebted to:
Blue Letter Bible. "Dictionary and Word Search for Petros (Strong's 4074)". Blue Letter Bible. 1996-2013. 27 Aug 2013. < http://www.blueletterbible.org/lang/lexicon/Lexicon.cfm?strongs=G4074 >
Blue Letter Bible. "Dictionary and Word Search for petra (Strong's 4073)". Blue Letter Bible. 1996-2013. 27 Aug 2013. < http://www.blueletterbible.org/lang/lexicon/Lexicon.cfm?strongs=G4073 >

CHAPTER 4
SEQUENCE OF
PROCLAMATION

"And, being assembled together with them, commanded them that they should not depart from Jerusalem, but wait for the promise of the Father, which, saith he, ye have heard of me" (Acts 1:4)

There was an order and sequence by which the Gospel of Jesus Christ was to be proclaimed since the ascension of Jesus Christ into heaven. This sequence was given by Jesus Christ himself. Even though the disciples were curious to know certain things even before those things were supposed to be known, Jesus commanded them to follow the sequence.

Firstly, they were asked not to be concerned of the time when the kingdom shall be restored to Israel. Secondly, they were asked to wait at Jerusalem to receive the promise of the Father and that promise was the coming of the Holy Spirit upon them.

Jesus promised to the disciples that they would not be left as orphans but The Comforter will be with them always. Thirdly, they were asked to go to one region first and then to another region and so on and after giving them the order, Jesus ascended into heaven.

The disciples did just as Jesus told them to do. They waited at Jerusalem and received the Holy Spirit and power came upon them. The Holy Spirit is right here as The Comforter.

The book of Acts is a systematic and detailed exposition written by Luke who wrote the Gospel of Luke. In continuation of all that Jesus taught until he ascended Luke also wrote about the infallible proofs Jesus left behind during the period of forty days between his resurrection from the dead and ascension into heaven.

Before ascension Jesus spoke to his disciples about the kingdom. The disciples were curious to know when he would restore the kingdom to Israel.

Jesus told them that it is not for them to know the times and seasons that the Father had put in his own power. He said to them that they would receive the power after the Holy Spirit comes upon them.

Then, they would be his witnesses both in Jerusalem and in all Judea and in Samaria and then in uttermost parts of the earth.

One noticeable fact here is the sequence that was to be followed for proclamation of the Gospel of Jesus Christ. First it would be in Jerusalem, his own place and to his own people, second it would be in Judea and Samaria, where Israelites and Gentiles lived, and lastly it would be to the utmost part of the earth; that is to every one.

These three stages are seen in Acts from Chapters 1-7, second from Chapters 8 to 12 and third from Chapters 13 to 28.

After Jesus spoke about these things to his disciples a cloud received Jesus as he ascended into heaven and they saw him no more. While the disciples looked steadfastly and watched two men stood by them in white apparel and said that Jesus who ascended into heaven will come back in the same way as he ascended.

Then they return to Mount of Olives which is at a distance of one Sabbath day's journey. (Sabbath day's journey is equivalent to seven and half furlongs and not a mile; this distance was based on conventional agreement among Jews as the distance that they can walk on a Sabbath day).

The disciples and others that were in upper room were one hundred and twenty in number Peter took leadership and spoke to them (Acts 1:6-15).

Mathias was numbered along with eleven disciples by lots to replace Judas Iscariot, who betrayed Jesus.

In the early days of proclamation of Gospel of Jesus Christ by the Apostles the power of God was seen clearly.

CHAPTER 5
KINGDOM OF GOD

The phrase 'Kingdom of God' refers to the God's kingdom that is the kingdom in which God reigns. It is the kingdom where God rules. Every kingdom will have a king and there is no kingdom without a king. The kingdom of God could be from the heart of a person who has accepted Jesus Christ as his/her personal Savior, or it could be the thousand year reign by Jesus Christ upon the earth after Lord Jesus has stepped on the Mount of Olives on His second coming.

A pointed and serious question from Jesus posed to Pharisees shows that there is kingdom of devil. Pharisees alleged that Jesus was casting away demons from those who were affected with evil spirits and then Jesus says to them if Satan cast out Satan he is divided against himself and every kingdom divided against itself is brought to desolation. He said when devils are cast out by the Spirit of God, then the kingdom of God is come into them.

"And Jesus knew their thoughts, and said unto them, Every kingdom divided against itself is brought to desolation; and every city or house divided against itself shall not stand: And if Satan cast out Satan, he is divided against himself; how shall then his kingdom stand? And if I by Beelzebub cast out devils, by whom do your children cast them out? therefore they shall be your judges. But if I cast out devils by the Spirit of God, then the kingdom of God is come unto you" (Matthew 12:25-28)

The Devil's kingdom started in the Garden of Eden, where the great Dragon, which was in the serpent, which was subtle "than any beast of the field which the LORD God had made" deceived Eve and then Adam, and ever since his endeavors without ceasing is to turn away man following God. The kingdom of God is the place where God wants everyone to come into, and it is what He wants to establish in everyone's heart.

God sent his message through Prophets, among whom, John the Baptist, was the last one, and people either rejected them or killed them. Finally, He sent His one and only Son, Lord Jesus Christ, into this world to save sinners. Jesus was the incarnate God Himself, in the form of servant, in the likeness of men. He preached repentance and said the 'kingdom of heaven' was at hand.

This obviously means accepting Jesus Christ will result in the establishment of the "Kingdom of God" in the heart of the one who accepted Him as the Lord. The Holy Spirit indwells the born again child of God, immediately one accepts Jesus Christ as one's personal Savior he enters into the "'kingdom of God". God rules in His Kingdom and His kingdom never ends.

When Jesus Christ comes on the clouds, the dead in Chris rise, and the living saints are caught up to be with Him for ever and ever. After the seven year Tribulation period Jesus Christ makes his advent upon the earth to reign for thousand years, during which period, the saints are caught up, also will reign along with Jesus Christ. He descends onto the Mount of Olives, and thereafter, there will be "Sheep and Goat Judgment", and then the thousand year reign starts upon the earth, and this is the literal "kingdom of heaven". This "kingdom of heaven" will have all those, who are saved during the period after Jesus descended onto earth. Satan is bound by an angel and casts him in to the bottomless pit. The Satan is released only after the thousand year reign by Jesus Christ ends. The phrase "Kingdom of God" also refers to this period of reign of Jesus Christ and the eternal Kingdom of God, in to which we the saints will be inherited.

It is worth noting that there are different gospels preached:

•The Gospel of the 'Kingdom of God' that deals with the fulfillment of Davidic-covenant that the 'kingdom shall be established for ever before thee: thy throne shall be established for ever'. (2 Samuel 7:16). This Kingdom of God includes the thousand year literal reign of Lord Jesus Christ from the throne of David in Jerusalem, as detailed in Zechariah 14:9 "And the LORD shall be king over all the earth: in that day shall there be one LORD, and his name one".

•The "Gospel of Christ" that deals with the Salvation of mankind that Apostle Paul spoke of, as the 'Grace of God', that Jesus died for our sins, and that He was raised from the dead. Jesus died and was raised for our justification and we are justified because of our belief in Him. "For we stretch not ourselves beyond our measure, as though we reached not unto you: for we are come as far as to you also in preaching the gospel of Christ" (2 Corinthians 10:14)

•The "Gospel" that is called "everlasting gospel", preached unto those, who did not believe in him, and who will pass through the "great tribulation" until the last days before the last judgment. "And I said unto him, Sir, thou knowest. And he said to me, These are they which came out of great tribulation, and have washed their robes, and made them white in the blood of the Lamb". (Revelation 7:14)

•The Gospel that is called "another gospel", which is the perversion of the Gospel of Christ. Christians are warned to be careful about this "another gospel" by the agents of Satan, who transforms himself as the angel of light. Apostle Paul writes about this gospel. "I marvel that ye are so soon removed from him that called you into the grace of Christ unto another gospel: Which is not another; but there be some that trouble you, and would pervert the gospel of Christ". (Galatians 1:6-7). False apostles calling themselves as apostles of Christ preach this gospel perverting the truth of the real gospel of Jesus that Apostle Paul calls as 'my gospel' in Romans 2:16, the gospel of Christ. However, "my gospel" is not to be understood as Paul's personal Gospel, but it is the same Gospel which Peter and others preached; that is of Lord Jesus Christ's death, burial and resurrection. Paul was contradicting those who were Judaizers, who insisted on circumcision for Gentiles to be saved.

Matthew 16:28 and Mark 9:1 seem to confuse believers as to who those standing there were, who Jesus was referring to as they do not taste the death till the 'Son of man' comes in his kingdom and what is the meaning of those two verses.. There are three views about the meaning of those verses. One section believes that Jesus was referring to the typical "kingdom of God" that He was going to show in his Transfiguration.

The second section believes that Jesus was referring to His second coming, and they are the one, who will be present in the days of Tribulation Period. The third section believes that he was referring to the spiritual kingdom that is established in the hearts of believers when they accept Jesus Christ as their personal Savior.

The phrases "kingdom of heaven" and "kingdom of God" are interchangeably used in the four Gospels while dealing with parallel themes. Jesus is indeed the King of the Jews. Jesus is not called the "King of the Church" but is called as "Head of the Church"

The Church came into existence as recorded in Acts Chapter 2 and not after the Acts 28 period. The earthly mission of Jesus was for restoration of kingdom to Jews, but then, because Jews rejected him as "Messiah" the salvation is extended to Gentiles as well.

The literal "kingdom of heaven" will come into existence when Lord Jesus Christ rules from the throne of David during the thousand-year-reign. The "kingdom of God" not only includes the millennial rule of Lord Jesus Christ but it has several aspects as we read in the parables mentioned in Matthew Chapter 13

"Be it known therefore unto you, that the salvation of God is sent unto the Gentiles, and that they will hear it" (Acts 28:28).

"Preaching the kingdom of God, and teaching those things which concern the Lord Jesus Christ, with all confidence, no man forbidding him". (Acts 28:31)

Going by the text from verse 23 to 31 of Acts Chapter 28 it is evident that Jews rejected the message from Apostle Paul. The message he expounded there was about the kingdom of God, both out of the Law of Moses, and out of the prophets from morning till evening and yet only some believed and some did not believe.

In the Gospel of Matthew the phrase "kingdom of heaven" used, and in parallel references in other Gospels this phrase appears as "kingdom of God".

Jesus indeed came in search of the lost sheep of Israel:

"These twelve Jesus sent forth, and commanded them, saying, Go not into the way of the Gentiles, and into any city of the Samaritans enter ye not: But go rather to the lost sheep of the house of Israel. And as ye go, preach, saying, The kingdom of heaven is at hand." (Matthew 10:5-7)

While it is true that Lord Jesus Christ sets up literal rule for thousand years on this earth at his second advent, the phrase used in four Gospels speak of the same kingdom, although the Matthew preferred to call it as "kingdom of heaven".

The message Paul spoke on different occasions before he finally settled to speak to the Gentiles was about Salvation which is free gift and is not associated with law and works. The message Peter spoke initially was about the "kingdom of God" to Jews before he spoke to Gentiles.

The kingdom, which was originally supposed to come into existence, if Jews accepted Jesus as their Messiah, was postponed to accommodate Gentiles in the Church. Jews rejected Jesus as their Messiah and this eventually paved the way for Gentiles to come into the Church. But then, was this a happening without the knowledge of God?

No, God had salvation to Gentiles in His plan and deliberately blinded the eyes of Jews. (Romans Chapters.9-11)

Jesus is not referred to as "King of the Church" but He is called "Head of the Church" and all the believers saved are His body and they are called the "Body of Christ".

The title of Jesus as "Christ" means that He is the Savior and He is the "Messiah" about whom the prophets prophesied. About Jesus was written in the books of Moses. The first one from Gentile to be saved was Cornelius, who was uncircumcised Gentile. The scriptures do not show anywhere that he was circumcised or grafted to become proselyte and to have the privileges of Jews.

Paul says in his epistles that Jews and Gentiles have equal privileges in the "Body of Christ". It was this mystery hidden in God the Gentiles should be partakers and become fellow heirs of Jews (Ephesians 3:2 and 3:6). This mystery was hidden in God even from the foundations of the earth.

Magi recognized Jesus as the King of the Jews. It is worth noticing that the wise men from the east came to Jerusalem to see the child Jesus and, even before they saw him, they recognized him as the King of the Jews born in Bethlehem.

King Herod was also troubled. He inquired of the child and, when wise men did not go back to him to give information that he needed, he was filled with anger, and slew all the children of the age up to two in Bethlehem, but by then Jesus was taken to Egypt by his parents. The wise men worshipped neither the mother of Jesus nor Joseph, but worshipped the child Jesus in Bethlehem.

"Saying, Where is he that is born King of the Jews? for we have seen his star in the east, and are come to worship him". (Matthew 2:2)

Jesus accepted worship as the King of Jews: In Matthew Chapter 21:1-11 there is a description as to how Jesus sent two disciples to get a donkey and a colt with her. He said to them that, if anyone asked them as to what they were doing, they should say to them that the Lord needs them. The disciples did as were commanded by Jesus.

Great multitude spread their garments in the way and some others sprayed branches of trees while Jesus rode on that donkey. The multitudes that went before and that followed him cried saying: "Hosanna to the Son of David: Blessed is he that cometh in the name of the Lord; Hosanna in the highest"

"Tell ye the daughter of Sion, Behold, thy King cometh unto thee, meek, and sitting upon an ass, and a colt the foal of an ass". (Matthew 21:5)

"Behold, the LORD hath proclaimed unto the end of the world, Say ye to the daughter of Zion, Behold, thy salvation cometh; behold, his reward is with him, and his work before him". (Isaiah 62:11)

Jesus stood before the governor and this was what He acknowledged.

"And Jesus stood before the governor: and the governor asked him, saying, Art thou the King of the Jews? And Jesus said unto him, Thou sayest" (Matthew 27:11)

However, when Jesus was accused of the chief priests and elders He answered nothing. This was because He was there to fulfill the desire of the Father and it pleased the Father to bruise Him, for our sins, in order that we may receive salvation.

Pilate thought he could release Jesus if he wants to, but he did not know that he could do nothing, without the power given to him from heaven. Jesus said to him that Pilate had no power at all over Jesus, except it was given to him from above.

"Then said Pilate unto him, Speak you not unto me? know you not that I have power to crucify you, and have power to release you? Jesus answered, You could have no power at all against me, except it were given you from above: therefore he that delivered me unto you has the greater sin". (John 19:10-11)

It was not by chance the inscription that Jesus was the 'King of Jews" was put on the cross on which Jesus was crucified but it was as God desired. Later, when the chief priests asked Pilate to change the writing as "he said, I am the King of the Jews", "Pilate answered, What I have written I have written" (John 19:22)

Then said the chief priests of the Jews to Pilate, Write not, The King of the Jews; but that he said, I am King of the Jews. (John 19:21)

The "kingdom of God" is not confined to only the thousand-year-reign of Lord Jesus Christ, but it has several aspects as we see in the parables recorded in Matthew Chapter 13.

Jesus did not show an unconcerned attitude towards Gentiles, even while He was seeking the lost sheep of Israel. The Canaanite woman, who was a Gentile, approached Jesus for a favor and although Jesus was initially reluctant to pay heed to her request, He granted her request when she showed faith in Him.

"And, behold, a woman of Canaan came out of the same coasts, and cried unto him, saying, Have mercy on me, O Lord, thou Son of David; my daughter is grievously vexed with a devil; but He answered her not a word. And his disciples came and besought him, saying, Send her away; for she crieth after us. But he answered and said, I am not sent but unto the lost sheep of the house of Israel. Then came she and worshipped him, saying, Lord, help me. But he answered and said, It is not meet to take the children's bread, and to cast it to dogs. And she said, Truth, Lord: yet the dogs eat of the crumbs which fall from their masters' table. Then Jesus answered and said unto her, O woman, great is thy faith: be it unto thee even as thou wilt. And her daughter was made whole from that very hour". (Matthew 15:22-28)

In another occasion when Jesus was speaking to the Samaritan woman, He spoke of everlasting life. But then, she was from the descendants of Jacob mixed with Gentiles based on this verse.

"Art thou greater than our father Jacob, which gave us the well, and drank thereof himself, and his children, and his cattle?" (John 4:12)

Earlier, Jesus also spoke to a centurion, and said that he had more faith than an Israelite: "When Jesus heard it, he marvelled, and said to them that followed, Verily I say unto you, I have not found so great faith, no, not in Israel". (Matthew 8:10)

That is to say that although the primary purpose of Jesus was to restore the kingdom to Children, and set up 'kingdom of God', He not only showed compassion towards Gentiles when He was on this earth, but He commanded His disciples to go the regions of Jerusalem first, and then to Judea and Samaria, and then to uttermost parts of the earth to preach the Gospel of Jesus Christ. (Acts 1:8)

Peter spoke of 'kingdom of God' initially as per the instructions given by Lord Jesus Christ before His ascension into heaven. He spoke to Jews first and then to Gentiles.

Paul also spoke to Jews first and then to Gentiles later. Paul was chosen to speak to Gentiles, but he ventured to Jews before he spoke to Gentiles. Some Jews accepted his message and some Jews rejected his message. This was fulfilled as was prophesied earlier. His commission is recorded in Acts 9:15

"But the Lord said unto him, Go thy way: for he is a chosen vessel unto me, to bear my name before the Gentiles, and kings, and the children of Israel"

"Make the heart of this people fat, and make their ears heavy, and shut their eyes; lest they see with their eyes, and hear with their ears, and understand with their heart, and convert, and be healed. (Isaiah 6:10)

"For the heart of this people is waxed gross, and their ears are dull of hearing, and their eyes have they closed; lest they should see with their eyes, and hear with their ears, and understand with their heart, and should be converted, and I should heal them". (Acts 28:27)

Thereafter, the message of salvation was sent out to Gentiles.

"I indeed baptize you with water unto repentance: but he that cometh after me is mightier than I, whose shoes I am not worthy to bear: he shall baptize you with the Holy Ghost and with fire" (Matthew 3:11)

Baptism with fire is meant for those who reject salvation. They will have their part in the lake of fire along with Satan and fallen angels. It was in Acts Chapter 2 that the Church began and Jesus became the head of the Church.

According to some 'kingdom of heaven' refers to the millennial kingdom of Jesus Christ, and 'kingdom of God' refers to the universal, including all moral intelligences willingly subject to the will of God, whether angels, the Church, or saints of past of future dispensations.

It is not a comfortable exposition that there are two different meanings one for "kingdom of heaven" and other for "kingdom of God". This exposition could be acceptable only if the parallel verses of the same theme in different Gospels had the same phrase; but it is not so.

Matthew, Mark, Luke and John's Gospels used the same theme at several points using different phrases interchangeably. There are many parallel verses in the four Gospels dealing with a particular theme yet with two different phrases. Moreover, angels do not need salvation nor will fallen angels be forgiven!

Few examples are as follows:

"From that time Jesus began to preach, and to say, Repent: for the kingdom of heaven is at hand" (Matthew 4:17)

"And saying, The time is fulfilled, and the kingdom of God is at hand: repent ye, and believe the gospel" (Mark 1:15) "But seek ye first the kingdom of God, and his righteousness; and all these things shall be added unto you" (Matthew 6:33)

"But rather seek ye the kingdom of God; and all these things shall be added unto you" (Luke 12:31)

"And said, Verily I say unto you, Except ye be converted, and become as little children, ye shall not enter into the kingdom of heaven" (Matthew 18:3)

"But when Jesus saw it, he was much displeased, and said unto them, Suffer the little children to come unto me, and forbid them not: for of such is the kingdom of God" (Mark 10:14)

"Verily I say unto you, Among them that are born of women there hath not risen a greater than John the Baptist: notwithstanding he that is least in the kingdom of heaven is greater than he" (Matthew 11:11)

"For I say unto you, Among those that are born of women there is not a greater prophet than John the Baptist: but he that is least in the kingdom of God is greater than he". (Luke 7:28)

CHAPTER 6
PARABLE OF THE SOWER

Lord Jesus Christ explained, in parables, how the 'kingdom of God' would be. When disciples asked Him why He spoke in parables, He said to them that the blessings to know the mysteries of the 'kingdom of heaven' were given unto them, but for others such depth of knowledge to know about the 'kingdom of God was not given. That is not to say that others were prohibited to know how the 'kingdom of God' is, nor does it mean that God hid any message from them, but it is to say that others do not understand, if the message is spoken directly, and, therefore, He spoke to them in illustrative methods, explaining His message to them, as also to His disciples, in parables.

"And the disciples came, and said unto him, Why speakest thou unto them in parables? He answered and said unto them, Because it is given unto you to know the mysteries of the kingdom of heaven, but to them it is not given" (Matthew 13:10-11)

KINGDOM OF GOD is like unto a sower, who went out to sow seeds in a field and when the seeds were sowed
- some fell by the wayside,
- some fell upon stony places,
- some fell among the thorns, and
- Some fell into the good ground.

- In first case, fowls came and devoured the seeds that fell by the wayside.

- In second case, there was not much earth; however the seeds sprung up into plants, but because there was no depth of the earth, and when the sun was up, they were scorched; and also because they did not have root, they withered away.
- In third case, thorns sprung up and choked the plants.
- In fourth case, the seeds that fell into the good ground, sprang up and brought forth fruit, some hundred-fold, some sixty-fold, and some thirty-fold.
  The field is the world; the seed is the word of God.

Jesus said: "Who hath ears to hear, let him hear. (Matthew 13:9)". He, then, explained the parable:

- When anyone hears the word of the kingdom, and does not understand what it is all about, then the wicked one comes, and snatches away that which was sown in his heart.
- He that received into stony places is the one, who hears the word, receives immediately with joy. As the root in him is not deep he is offended very quickly.
- He who receives the word of the kingdom as do thorns receive seeds, endures for a while, but when he falls under pressures of the cares of this world, deceitfulness of riches, they chokes the word in his heart, and he becomes unfruitful.
- However, he that receives the word of the kingdom , as does the good ground receives

seeds, is fruitful and brings forth, some hundred-fold, some sixty-fold, and some thirty-fold.

CHAPTER 7
SEEK YE FIRST THE
KINGDOM OF GOD

But seek you first the kingdom of God, and his righteousness; and all these things shall be added unto you. (Matthew 6:33)

As we read through the life history of Joseph, we see that he was elevated while his offenders were thrown into insecurity and fear for future. God's child, will never be left to be without hope, but will be elevated, while his offenders will be thrown in to insecurity and fear for their future. God assures his children that when they seek the Kingdom of God; all their needs will be fulfilled.

I would not like you to think that life of a child of God will be bed of roses! No! The child of God will face as many troubles as others do or even more; but there is hope that God will do everything for good for those who are called according to his purpose.

Psalmist said that he has not seen any child of God begging for bread! There is peace of mind and there is comfort and deliverance from problems always. God does everything good for those who believe in Him.

"I have been young, and now am old; yet have I not seen the righteous forsaken, nor his seed begging bread". (Psalms 37:25)

Those who seek pleasures of this world are not thinking in terms of securing treasures in heaven.

We see how insecure Joseph's brothers and Jacob were feeling because of their worry about future, even though they were the children of God. Seeing the circumstances around them, they were worried. Joseph's brothers felt insecure, because of their guilt feeling that God was punishing them for selling their own brother. Jacob, in his old age was worried about his children and his own future.

In fact, as we read through the story we find that everything works for good for those who are called according to his purpose.

"And we know that all things work together for good to them that love God, to them who are the called according to his purpose." Romans 8:28

It was God's plan that there should be abundance for seven years and famine for the next seven years that should follow immediately the seven years of abundance. It was, in His plan that someone, whom he loved and thought would best fit for the disposition of food for seven years of famine, should be one from Jacob's family and that was Joseph.

It was in His plan that the blessed one, Jacob, whom He called, Israel, should survive the severe famine. It was His plan that during that period of seven years of famine, someone from the family of Jacob should be in Egypt to provide food for Jacob's family.

Even when all this was happening at the behest of God, the children of Israel were worried about their survival, future, and, therefore, indicted themselves of having sold their brother, Joseph, many years ago. They did not know that their food was already stored for them by God many years before they knew about it. They were worried as to what their destiny would be.

God's children have a great a hope as we read in Matthew 6:34, where Jesus expressly, said "Take therefore no thought for the morrow: for the morrow shall take thought for the things of itself. Sufficient unto the day is the evil thereof".

CHAPTER 8
PUBLIC MINISTRY OF LORD JESUS CHRIST

"This beginning of miracles did Jesus in Cana of Galilee, and manifested forth his glory; and his disciples believed on him". John 2:11

Jesus started his ministry with the miracle that he did in Cana of Galilee, where he manifested forth his glory in order that his disciples and others there would believe that he was the Messiah. Jesus came into this world relinquishing the glory that he had with the Father and took the form of man. While on this world he lived like an ordinary man, yet with full divine power.

Jesus did miracles that were unknown to the natives of Galilee, Nazareth, Capernaum and the surrounding areas. Very few miracles are only recorded in the Scriptures.

Jesus did many miracles according to John 21:25 but very few are recorded that are sufficient for unbelievers to know about his power and glory that he had with the Father. In the miracle that Jesus did at Cana, where he turned water into wine, he manifested forth his glory. For the disciples, whom he called from the general and poor folk, to follow him, this miracle was a great consolation and rest on him in faith that he was the true Messiah. They believed on him.

Jesus was walking by the Sea of Galilee, where he saw two brothers; Simon called Peter and Andrew his brother, who were casting a net into the sea to catch fishes. Jesus asked them to follow him promising that he would make them fishers of men. (Matthew 4:18-20). They immediately left their nets and followed him. This miracle that Jesus did at Cana was the first one in his ministry when he was about thirty years of age.

CHAPTER 9
SALVATION TO THE JEWS

The life of Moses contributes to an interesting study as it stands out unique in comparison with the life of Lord Jesus Christ. Moses had three major roles to perform, the first of which was to be the leader of Israelites, the second of which was to give law to the children of Israel and the third of which was to mediate between them and God.

Jesus came into this world as the way, the truth and the life, to redeem mankind from their sinful nature. He gave the mankind the beatitudes as found in Matthew Chapter 5, 6 and 7.

Jesus gave two great commandments as recorded in Mark 12:30-31 "And thou shalt love the Lord thy God with all thy heart, and with all thy soul, and with all thy mind, and with all thy strength: this is the first commandment. And the second is like, namely this, Thou shalt love thy neighbour as thyself. There is none other commandment greater than these".

These two commandments contain the essence of all the Ten Commandments. Jesus came to be a mediator between the Father and us. Moses was the deliverer of God's children physically, while the mission of Jesus was to deliver spiritually of His people Jews first. Since Jews rejected him as Messiah the Gentiles had the privilege to approach God. But then this salvation to Gentiles was not planned all of a sudden.

Apostle Paul says in Ephesians Chapter 3 and Romans chapter 11 that God's plan to give salvation to Gentiles was hidden in God from the foundation of the world and was revealed in the New Testament.

"For I would not, brethren, that ye should be ignorant of this mystery, lest ye should be wise in your own conceits; that blindness in part is happened to Israel, until the fulness of the Gentiles be come in" (Romans 11:25)

"But now hath he obtained a more excellent ministry, by how much also he is the mediator of a better covenant, which was established upon better promises". (Hebrews 8:6) The Old covenants included in them the shadows of new things to come.

Old Testament law was stringent in nature, and the law demanded unconditional obedience. It was hard to keep the law that is in the Old Testament. In the New Testament God's abundant grace is available. Man by confessing his sins to God and accepting Jesus as the Lord will receive eternal life.

Repentance of sins to Jesus and accepting him as the Lord is sufficient to be saved. Lord Jesus Christ is the only mediator between man and the Father.

CHAPTER 10
LAW AND GRACE

Apostle Paul admonishes Galatians in no uncertain terms for believing in works associated with salvation. The word he used is 'bewitched'. He was not only asking them as to who has cast a spell over their understanding or enchantment, or fascinated them about their belief that law would save them and works were associated with their salvation, but called them 'fools' (Galatians 3:1) for such belief as they hold that law and works could save them.

The word 'fools' used here does not demean them that they lack wisdom and prudence, but he demeans their misunderstanding that they must do something under the law to God in recompense to what he has done for us. The meaning of 'fool' here was similar to what Jesus meant in Matthew 7:26.

The whole chapter of Galatians 3 deals with this subject of law versus grace. He not only questions them if there is anyone in the world, who is perfect in flesh, but also provides answers to his questions that no one could be saved by the law and works associated with it. He goes on to say that only faith in Jesus Christ, who redeemed us from the curse of the law, could save us.

Abraham believed God, and it was reckoned unto him as righteousness. He says that the children, who are of faith, are the children of Abraham. The Scriptures foresaw that God would justify the heathen through faith, and made available to us, the Word, through preaching, and made available this preaching even before the proclamation of the gospel unto Abraham, that in him shall all nations be blessed. Obviously, this indicates that those, who are of faith in Christ, are blessed with faithful Abraham.

Apostle goes on, further, saying that those, who, think that they are still under the works of the law, subject themselves to be under the curse, inasmuch as it written in the Scriptures that whoever continues to believe in becoming perfect by obedience to the commandments written in the law is cursed; no one can be justified before God under the law.

The just shall live by faith and it is certain that the law is not of faith, but whosoever, tries to believe that law would save them would live by them, and would be under the curse.

Lord Jesus indeed came to save his own, but when they rejected him, salvation was made available for Gentiles. No doubt this was in the plan of God, and this mystery was revealed in Romans 11:6-11. He came into this world to provide a way out from these stringent laws, and provided a way for everyone, that by faith in him a person is saved by grace.

Jesus was hung on the cross and bore our sins so that we may not be cursed. It is written that 'cursed is everyone that hangeth on a tree'. He came into this world so that the blessing of Abraham would be available for Gentiles through him, so that the gentiles also may receive the promise of the Spirit through faith.

There seems to arise a question in the minds of those, who have no good understanding about law versus grace as to why then God gave law in the first place and then asked us to be under 'grace'.

Apostle Paul writes that the law is not against the promises of God, but it was given in order that man may understand that the transgressions he committed cannot be forgiven by law, which only points out the guilt of a person. Under the law priest had to offer sacrifice first and then offer a sacrifice for the person, who is guilty. If law could make a person righteous the life truly righteousness should have been by law, but the Scripture has concluded all under sin.

The promise by faith of Lord Jesus Christ was made available only to those who believe. The law was our schoolmaster in order to teach us the way unto Jesus, who is the only mediator, and we can be justified only by faith in him. After Jesus had become propitiation for us, it is not required of us to do what is to be done under the law in order to have salvation; but faith in him alone is enough and that is to say that we are no longer under schoolmaster.

As many as have believed and accepted Jesus Christ as personal Savior and Lord, have put on Christ, irrespective of whether they are Jew or Greek, bonded or free, or male or female. All those, who are saved with the precious blood of Jesus Christ are one in him and we belong to him and we are Abraham's seed by faith and have inherited the promises.

What is Redemption?

Redemption, in the context of New Testament doctrine, is getting something back for the price paid; in other words, setting forth a sinner free from the bondage of sin with the price paid by Jesus Christ on the cross. It is to deliver by paying price.

There are three things that take place in the process of redemption. It is buying something that was under bondage. It was setting free from the bondage and it is freeing from that bondage. This is what exactly what Christ did on the cross on behalf of sinner.

Every man is under the bondage of sin from the time he is born in the womb of his mother. Scripture says, there is no one righteous, and anyone who does not accept this fact is making the writer of the Scripture a liar -- '1 John 1:10 If we say that we have not sinned, we make him a liar, and his word is not in us. '

The man under the bondage of sin needs deliverance. This is what Christ did on the cross by dying in the stead of sinner taking upon himself the sins of the sinner fulfilling the law. Every man, who is freed from the bondage, needs to be delivered just as a product or animal is taken out of the market place and freed.

This is what Jesus did by freeing from the bondage of sin, and delivering us from the penalty of sin, which is death. Our bodies perish and we rise in glory with glorified bodies. While the bodies still lie in the grave and perish, the soul of a believer is eternally present with the Lord Jesus Christ right from the movement is gives up his earthly life.

Romans 7:13 Was then that which is good made death unto me? God forbid. But sin, that it might appear sin, working death in me by that which is good; that sin by the commandment might become exceeding sinful.

The law pointed out sin, but the grace delivered us from the bondage of sin. Accepting Jesus as the Lord and Savior will set a sinner free from the bondage of sin, and entitles him to have eternal life.

CHAPTER 11
THE LOVE OF GOD"

"Who shall lay any thing to the charge of God's elect? It is God that justifieth. Who is he that condemneth? It is Christ that died, yea rather, that is risen again, who is even at the right hand of God, who also maketh intercession for us. Who shall separate us from the love of Christ? shall tribulation, or distress, or persecution, or famine, or nakedness, or peril, or sword? As it is written, For thy sake we are killed all the day long; we are accounted as sheep for the slaughter. Nay, in all these things we are more than conquerors through him that loved us. For I am persuaded, that neither death, nor life, nor angels, nor principalities, nor powers, nor things present, nor things to come, Nor height, nor depth, nor any other creature, shall be able to separate us from the love of God, which is in Christ Jesus our Lord ".

Adam transgressed God's commandment when he ate of the fruit of the knowledge of good and evil brought to him by the woman after she was deceived by the serpent. The serpent was 'more subtil than any beast of the field which the LORD God had made '.

Adam brought upon himself and his posterity the condemnation of death. It was the consequence of imputation of guilt to him because he transgressed the commandment of God. Man needed reconciliation and forgiveness. Jesus, the Son of God came into this world, took upon himself man's sin, died on the cross. Jesus, whom God hath raised up, having loosed the pains of death: because it was not possible that he should be holden of it. (Acts 2 :24). Jesus ascended into heaven and is now seated on the right of the Majesty.

Whosoever believes this fact will have eternal life. For if by one man's offence death reigned by one; much more they which receive abundance of grace and of the gift of righteousness shall reign in life by one, Jesus Christ. Romans 5 :17

Apostle Paul writes in Galatians 3:24 "Wherefore the law was our schoolmaster to bring us unto Christ, that we might be justified by faith " The Law was given to Moses and for those under Old Testament Covenant. The believer in Christ is not asked here to disregard the Law, but is asked not to be under its bondage, because law cannot save any person. The law brings a sinner in to condemnation.

A New Testament believer is not under the bondage of law. The Scriptures say that if anyone is bent upon keeping the law he needs to keep all the commandments, which is virtually impossible.

The message is clearly not to be disobedient to law or disregard the law. The message is clearly that of emphasizing the fact that it is impossible for any human to keep the law that was given by God, and be justified; the justification was possible only through the blood that was shed on the cross, of Jesus.

The Old Testament Law was abolished when Jesus was crucified on the cross. The Old Testament Law was nailed to the cross as we read in Colossians 2 :14 "Blotting out the handwriting of ordinances that was against us, which was contrary to us, and took it out of the way, nailing it to his cross " Romans 10 :4 "For Christ is the end of the law for righteousness to every one that believeth ".

If anyone still believes in the Old Testament Laws, then Christ is no effect to him inasmuch as the Scripture says, 'whosoever of you are justified by the law; ye are fallen from grace '. All those, who were in Old Testament period, have seen that no one could keep the law perfectly.

The law always pointed to the sin, and showed the guilt of a person. It always demanded works, and condemned. Even before the foundation of the world God knew that man cannot keep the law, and needs a savior.

The law was given to him to show in the future days to come that after the law was given and after it is seen that men have failed to keep the law, man should be made to understand that he needs grace and nothing but grace.

No amount of good works could save a person; but the salvation is received by sinner only by laying faith in Jesus and faith alone in him saves a person.

More references : Jeremiah 31 :31-34, 1 Corinthians 10 :1-4, Romans 15 :4, Galatians 5 :4, Romans 7 :4-6, Ephesians 2 :15

"Whom God hath set forth to be a propitiation through faith in his blood, to declare his righteousness for the remission of sins that are past, through the forbearance of God" (Romans 3:25)

"I and my Father are one" (John 10:30)

CHAPTER 12
JUSTIFICATION

1 Corinthians 1:30 But of him are ye in Christ Jesus, who of God is made unto us wisdom, and righteousness, and sanctification, and redemption

Justification is the declaration that our Lord and Savior Jesus Christ makes before the Father about a sinner, who believes in Jesus Christ and accepts him as his personal Savior. The sinner, who confesses him as the 'Lord' is justified by him as righteous because Christ has borne the sins of sinner on the cross of Calvary and made him righteous.

The justification originates in and through the grace. It is by grace through faith in him that a sinner is saved. No amount of good works can save a person, nor can justify him as righteous before God.

 "Being justified freely by his grace through the redemption that is in Christ Jesus" Romans 3:24

It is judicial act that Jesus has performed on the cross. He paid the price for the redemption of sinner. He died in the stead of a sinner. That is how he justifies the sinner as righteous before the Father. All that a sinner needs to do is to accept the fact that Jesus Christ has died on the cross in his stead and rose from the dead on the third day.

It is by faith in Jesus as the redeemer that a sinner is saved and no charge is laid against him, irrespective of what gross sin he/she has committed. Every sin, except blasphemy of Holy Spirit, is pardonable by God. Christ has established the law by taking upon himself the penalty of sin, which is death.

As believers in Christ we have blessed hope that after death we will have a glorified bodies that are not made of hands but that which will be with the Lord eternally in the heavens. The body that we have now is made of dust and we groan in this body to be clothed to hide nakedness, in contrast to the glorified bodies that we will have in heaven.

Our bodies are made with the dust from this earth and, therefore, suffer sickness and decay in contrast to the glorified bodies that do not suffer any sickness or decay in eternity. This is the reason why we believers are happy to be absent in this body so that we can be present eternally with the Lord, and, therefore, we do not fear death. In this body we labor to earn for our life on this earth, but in eternity we are blessed with the rewards that our Lord gives us for the works that we have done for him on this earth.

Jesus died for our sake, and rose again from the dead giving us the blessed hope that even though we die we will rise once in glorified bodies.

"So also is the resurrection of the dead. It is sown in corruption ; it is raised in incorruption : (1 Corinthians 15 :42)

"Therefore if any man be in Christ, he is a new creature : old things are passed away ; behold, all things are become new ". (2 Corinthians 5 :17)

"The Price is already paid for" John 19:30

When Jesus therefore had received the vinegar, he said, It is finished: and he bowed his head, and gave up the ghost.

This is one of the seven sayings of Jesus when he was on the cross of Calvary. He was despised and rejected by man

This is the fulfillment of prophesy that is written in Isaiah 53 :4 -7 "Surely he hath borne our griefs, and carried our sorrows: yet we did esteem him stricken, smitten of God, and afflicted. But he was wounded for our transgressions; he was bruised for our iniquities: the chastisement of our peace was upon him; and with his stripes we are healed. All we like sheep have gone astray; we have turned every one to his own way ; and the LORD hath laid on him the iniquity of us all. He was oppressed, and he was afflicted, yet he opened not his mouth: he is brought as a lamb to the slaughter, and as a sheep before her shearers is dumb, so he openeth not his mouth ".

He was led like a lamb to be slaughtered. His hands and feet were nailed. He was numbered with the transgressors his death.

Isaiah 53 :10 "Yet it pleased the LORD to bruise him; he hath put him to grief: when thou shalt make his soul an offering for sin, he shall see his seed, he shall prolong his days, and the pleasure of the LORD shall prosper in his hand. " His blood was paid as price for our redemption. There was nothing more, nor is anything more to be done any person for receiving salvation.

It is just the faith in him as Lord and Savior is the requirement to have everlasting life. Jesus took upon himself our infirmities and sin so that we may have everlasting life by accepting as our Lord. It pleased the Father to bruise him so that we may receive salvation. There is no price attached to that invaluable gift that is made available for us. The price is already paid.

Admonishing Galatians time and again, Apostle Paul continues to emphasize on the fact that there is salvation only in Jesus through faith by grace and not by law and works associated with it.

Getting entangled with law and with the thought that they need to do something to be saved, is tantamount to be under the yoke of bondage, he says. About, circumcision, he condemns it and says that if anyone is of the belief that circumcision is necessary for salvation or for justification, the obsession of such thought will not profit them and Christ and his blood is of nothing to them.

Everyone, who is circumcised becomes debtor to the whole law and Christ and his sacrifice has nothing for him. We are reckoned as righteous only by faith in Jesus and by his grace. Neither circumcision nor un-circumcision avails anything to a believer in Christ.

Walking in the Spirit and hatred of lust of the flesh are necessary on the part of a believer to lead a holy life. One great truth a believer has to understand is that flesh lusts against the Spirit and the Spirit against the flesh and these are contrary to each other. If we are of the Spirit and are led by the Spirit we are not under the law and would not yield to the desires of the flesh.

After having known of the love of God through His one only begotten son, Jesus, why would we turn yet unto beggarly elements like observing the days, months, times and years, and be subject again to be under the bondage of the law?

When the price for our sin and redemption is already paid for, why would we turn again to work for our salvation by ourselves? Salvation is available free of cost; the price is already paid for. All that is needed on the part of sinner is to believe that Jesus paid the price of his sin on the cross, and that he needs to believe in his/her heart this fact and accept him as his/her personal Savior.

Apostle Paul blesses those, who do not voluntarily subject themselves to be under the yoke of law, but accept Christ's death upon the cross. He says fulfilling the law of Christ is more important than that of the Old Testament laws. No one should boast of himself nor glory himself/herself, but everyone should glorify Lord Jesus Christ, whose marks were borne by not only Apostle Paul but all those, who realize the efficacy of the blood of Lord Jesus Christ.

Paul's feels as if he was under the travail of child birth to explain to Galatians the difference between law and grace, and how hard it is to be under law rather than accept 'grace' alone as the way for salvation. He calls them, now, 'my little children', and try to explain to them about the implications in believing that law and works only would save them.

Galatians were under the erroneous belief that law and works only can save them. They desired to take pride in a list of rules they prescribed for them and as they keep the rules they would consider them as perfect. That, in other words, renders a notion that man can earn his own salvation by keeping a set of rules, like being good and doing good etc.

These things help men to be good men but would not secure salvation that is available free of cost as a result of belief in the works of Jesus, the Son of God, did for men. He came down into this world to redeem us from the bondage of sin, and, therefore, took upon himself, our transgressions and died for our sake.

The fruits of the Holy Spirit are love, joy, peace, longsuffering, gentleness, goodness, faith, Meekness, temperance. A saved man will have in him the Spirit of God and will have the fruits of the Holy Spirit.

However, possession of these good qualities without accepting Jesus as 'Lord' will not make us a man eligible to have eternal life. The only way to have eternal life is to believe in the efficacy of the blood of Jesus Christ and accept the fact that he died in our stead on the cross.

Paul explains to Galatians, just as a matured man explaining to children that all those who believe that law can save them are like those, who are of 'bondwoman' and all those who believe in the 'grace' of Jesus are like those, who are of free woman. He quotes from Old Testament the things that have happened in *Abram*'s life as described in Genesis 16th Chapter.

Sarai sent her handmaid, Hagar to sleep with Abram, and a son was born. It was legalism on the part of *Sarai* and *Abram* a method that finds a way out for them.

Later a son was born to **Abraham** and his wife **Sarah** as a consequence of the promise of God to them. This son of the promise of God was of faith in God and His grace.

The son, who was born to Hagar was of the flesh, and the son born of promise to Sarai, was blessed. The posterity of bondwoman are still under bondage of Mosaic law, and the posterity of the free woman, who are supposed to be free from the bondage of Mosaic law, have unfortunately, embraced the law and works as their way for salvation, rejected Messiah as their Savior, and are still under the bondage of law.

Paul desires that everyone should embrace the belief that it is by 'grace' of God that saves a man. Paul allegorizes this to the Jerusalem, which is above all, that consists of the posterity of Isaac, born of **Sarah** and that 'grace' alone saves a person. The legalists still insist that it is right to be under the law and keep the law to be saved. Such legalism will lead to the belief that there is no justification by the grace of God, but their own works will lead them to have eternal life.

Speaking of law and grace and the firm belief of Jews in their belief of laws plus works for their salvation rather than depending on pure mercy of God by grace through faith, another point that could we could meditate is on the fact as to why God did not have his own people, Jews, realize this so quickly that pure grace from God is alone sufficient for their salvation.

There is enough reason, as we understand, that God not only wanted his own people, Jews, to have their salvation, but also Gentiles to enjoy that privilege of calling him as 'Abba, Father'. .

Apostle Paul wonders if God cast away his people and immediately reaffirms that it was not so, because he was also of the seed of Abraham, of the tribe of Benjamin. God did not cast away his people, whom he foreknew. Even when Elias was taking pride in himself that he was alone available to intercede on behalf of Israel, God says to him, that he had reserved seven thousand men unto him, who could intercede on behalf of Israel. If the salvation, therefore, is by 'grace', then it is not by 'works'.

What then happened exactly that their attitude and belief has not changed yet? Yes, it is because God blinded their eyes and gave them spiritual slumber, that they should not see and that they may not have ears for hearing unto this day. Have Israel stumbled that they should fall then?

Apostle Paul himself answers these questions (Romans 11th Chapter) that God did not blind them or made them deaf because of they were stumbling blocks nor is it because they have stumbled, but because of the desire God had that everyone in the world, irrespective of Jews or Gentiles be saved and have eternal life.

Pillars are the strength of monuments and on the pillars are seen inscriptions or designs that either bring to us some remembrance of those, who responsibly raised them, or help us admire their beauty. Heaven does not need any pillar to support it, but the new Jerusalem, that John saw in his vision coming down from heaven was like a bride adorned for her bridegroom.

In this New Jerusalem were seen the pillars on which were written the names of those, who served the living

God, and the names of who those, who they served and represented. Some in the Church at Philadelphia (Rev 3:3-5) had not defiled their garments and they were worthy to receive blessings. God promised that he who overcomes shall walk with Him.

Those that overcome stand for the living God, and they are like pillars in the temple of God, and on them are written the names, such as 'name of my God', 'name of the city of my God', which is 'new Jerusalem', and His new name. (Rev 21:2-5)

This is the difference between the earthly Jerusalem and the new Jerusalem that comes down from heaven. John saw a new heaven and a new earth after the first heaven and the first earth passed away and there was no more sea.

In this New Jerusalem there was not seen any difference between Jews or Gentiles, but those who were there were all one in Christ. They had put on righteousness of Christ as their garments. They had received Jesus as their personal Savior and Lord by grace through faith in him.

More than anyone taking of airs of his belonging to any clan the important fact that is to be borne in mind is that it is the grace of God that saves a man. No man needs precious metals such as gold and silver to earn a place in new Jerusalem, but all that a man needs is to have simple faith in Jesus, the Son of God and make him Lord of his/her life. God wipes away their tears.

There shall be no more death, no more sorrow, no more crying and no more pain. God shall give freely to all that thirst for such a life the fountain of life. He who overcomes the world and the temptations therein shall inherit the blessings from God and he shall be His son.

Apostle Paul explains elaborately the plan of God for the salvation of Gentiles in Romans 11th Chapter. It was not because Israel have stumbled nor because they were stumbling blocks to anybody that their eyes were blinded and their ears were short of hearing and understanding who their Messiah was and what exactly they needed to do for their salvation. They always insisted that because God had done something for them they owe to God something that they essentially do and such recompense only will fetch their salvation. It is because of their misunderstanding that salvation is come unto the Gentiles.

Paul warns Gentiles that they are like grafted wild olive tree in the places, where the branches of the natural branches were broken off. The Gentiles are partakers of the root and fatness of the natural olive tree. Therefore, he says, Gentiles should not be of high-minded, but fear.

The branches of the natural olive tree were broken off by God himself, because of their unbelief, and the Gentiles, who were like wild olive trees have, now, the sap and blessings from the root of the natural olive tree.

If Gentiles were to be high-minded and take pride in themselves or their own merits, God will not hesitate to chastise them. If God did not spare the natural branches of the olive tree would he tolerate the grafted olive tree; never!

In the book of Hosea the pathetic condition of Israel is seen. Israel, who had been blessed and to whom were the blessings and covenants given, continually fell from the presence of the Lord. In the sight of the Lord, who asked Hosea to marry a prostitute, Israel was similar to Prostitute, dishonest with her infidelity.

God, who was like husband to them had to see her deviation from the honesty and loyalty, had to chastise them time and again. The Lord goes on to say that they are not his people, and he is not their God. He was like a frustrated husband trying to bring them to the path of salvation, yet they erred time and again. This was the reason, why God had to extend salvation to the Gentiles, thus making Jews and Gentiles one in Christ.

It was not a mystery that the Gentiles should be saved but one mystery was certainly there that God would form Church consisting of Jews and Gentiles, and that Church is above Jews and Gentiles. This purpose was hidden in God until it was revealed to us in Ephesians 2nd Chapter.

The Church is the body of Christ. In this Church are no differences as to who is Jew and who is Gentile, but everyone has similar status. In this Church is seen no more distinction of earthly differences of race, ethnicity, clan, color, and nationality. It is the blood of Jesus that saves a man from being condemned to death and eternal destruction. It is the water that Jesus gives that becomes living water for the sinner. It is the life that Jesus gives to sinner that becomes eternal life.

God in his mercy and love for us quickened us in spirit together with Christ and by grace we are saved. He has given us the privilege to be seated together in heavenly places in Christ Jesus.

Faith in him alone saved us and not of any good works in us or by us. If the salvation is by works, then anybody could boast of himself/herself by doing good works that he is worthy to receive salvation by himself, and of his good works. This renders the sacrifice of Jesus of null effect.

The very purpose of Jesus coming into this world was to bear on himself, the sins of the world so that whoever believes in him could be saved. If good works of any man could save him, then Christ need not have come to this world. There is a fundamental error in believing that good works of any man would save him from his sins. "We are his workmanship, created in Christ Jesus unto good works".

This was in the plan of God even before the foundation of the world. The good works of a man will not save him but in Christ Jesus we will do good works as a result of having the fruit of the Holy Spirit. "We were without Christ, and aliens from the commonwealth of Israel" We had no hope of having salvation but in the blood of Jesus Christ we are made one.

Apostle Paul emphasizes in Romans 6th chapter that sin shall not have dominion over a born-again child because he/she is not under the law, but under grace. Those who seek to do good works and earn salvation by their own works have nullified the importance of blood of Jesus Christ and in their lives the blood of Jesus Christ that cleanses the sin has no value for them. They diligently keep doing good works neglecting the repeated emphasis from the Lord Jesus Christ that his blood saves and gives eternal life to all those, who go to him and accept him as the Lord.

After having been delivered from the bondage of sin by grace through faith should a child of God keep sinning because he is under the grace but not under law? Paul very firmly says, "God forbid".

Never should a child of God return to sin and lose blessings from God. Salvation is not lost for those who are saved in the blood of Jesus Christ\; however, the Scripture does not endorse repeated sinning. God will surely chide and chastise the one that falls repeatedly into sin and seeks grace time and again.

Should we not consider the fact that if he yield to sin we are servants to sin and sin becomes our master; we are under grace and we should remain servants to our Lord and be of obedience to righteousness.

We were, once, servants of sin, but after accepting Jesus as our master, we have become servants of righteousness. We have our fruit unto holiness, and everlasting life. The law has concluded all of us under sin, but the gift of God is eternal life through Lord Jesus Christ.

John Chapter 10 deals with the subject of the relationship between him and those who have accepted him as the Lord. The comparison of the shepherd and his flock with Jesus his beloved ones is that Jesus is good shepherd. He is the door and there is no other way to the pasture.

A thief does not enter the sheepfold by the door, but enters climbing the wall and entering some other way. Jesus said, if any man enters by Him he shall be saved. A good shepherd gives life for his flock, but a hireling does not give his life. Hireling would run away leaving sheep helpless, when he encounters some danger.

On the contrary, a good shepherd will leave ninety nine sheep aside and seek after the lost one sheep, and finds it and brings it back to the flock. Jesus is our good shepherd. 'I am the good shepherd, and know my sheep, and am known of mine '.

The word, 'know ' here shows the love that the sheep show toward their good shepherd, whom they trust and obey. Jesus asserts here that he is the good shepherd, who will not let his sheep be stolen by his enemy. He would leave ninety nine sheep aside for some time to go in search of one lost or backslidden sheep to bring it back to join the ninety nine.

John 10:27-30 'My sheep hear my voice, and I know them, and they follow me: And I give unto them eternal life; and they shall never perish, neither shall any man pluck them out of my hand. My Father, which gave them me, is greater than all; and no man is able to pluck them out of my Father's hand. I and my Father are one. John 10:14 'I am the good shepherd, and know my sheep, and am known of mine '.

The word, 'know ' here shows the love that the sheep show toward their good shepherd, whom they trust and obey. Jesus asserts here that he is the good shepherd, who will not let his sheep be stolen by his enemy. He would leave ninety nine sheep aside for some time to go in search of one lost or backslidden sheep to bring it back to join the ninety nine.

John 10:27-30 'My sheep hear my voice, and I know them, and they follow me: And I give unto them eternal life; and they shall never perish, neither shall any man pluck them out of my hand. My Father, which gave them me, is greater than all; and no man is able to pluck them out of my Father's hand. I and my Father are one. John 10:14'

Jesus Christ is the Son of God and very God Himself. Jesus said, in John 10:30 'I and my Father are one '. He said in John 16:15 'All things that the Father hath are mine: therefore said I, that he shall take of mine, and shall shew it unto you '. He said in John 17:11 'And now I am no more in the world, but these are in the world, and I come to thee. Holy Father, keep through thine own name those whom thou hast given me, that they may be one, as we are '.

Apostle Paul wrote about Jesus Christ in Colossians 1:15-18 'Who is the image of the invisible God, the firstborn of every creature: For by him were all things created, that are in heaven, and that are in earth, visible and invisible, whether they be thrones, or dominions, or principalities, or powers: all things were created by him, and for him: And he is before all things, and by him all things consist. And he is the head of the body, the church: who is the beginning, the firstborn from the dead; that in all things he might have the preeminence.

When we think of the sin King David did by committing adultery with Bathsheba we cannot think of any reason why God would not forgive our sins. David was blessed one, God chose him to be King, yet one day when [2Sam 11th Chapter] saw from the roof of his home, a beautiful woman named Bathsheba washing herself.

David sent messengers and took her, and committed sin with her. He did not end his iniquity there but conspired and got her husband, Uriah, killed in the battle. God punished David for his sin. David's son from Bathsheba died, and David had to pay great penalty for his sin. Yet, when David repented of his sin, He had compassion on him and forgave him, and restored him.

Jesus became poor for us even though he was rich in his glory and was with the Father from eternity. He said he is the beginning and he is the end; he is the Alpha and Omega. He is the creator of this universe, he owns everything, every creation and he is the King of kings, he is the Lord or lords, and he is the God of gods.

Lord Jesus was in the form of God and did not think it robbery to be to equal with God, but made himself of no repute, took the form of servant, and became like a man and dwelt among us. He was born of the Virgin Mary, by the works of Holy Spirit, and was laid in a manger. He was raised in a poor family. His earthly parents offered turtle doves as offerings (Luke 2:24), which was a provision made for poor and those, who could not offer bull or goat as sacrifice as per Old Testament Law. In Colossians 1st Chapter verses 15 to 17, there is a clear description that Jesus the creator. He is the image of the invisible God, the first born of every creature, and by him were all things created; yet we see that he took the form of man for our sake. He testified, in Luke 9:58 how poor he was on this earth.

All this was took place because Jesus became a sacrifice on our behalf, when he took upon himself, our curse, our sin and shed his precious blood upon the cross of Calvary.

The salvation is received by his 'grace' through faith in him that he died and rose for our sake, and by accepting his as 'Lord '. He offered himself on the cross so that we may have riches in him. The earthly riches are not true riches. What if a man earns whole earth his soul? We are saved by his precious blood and not of any of our works. We are not purchased by gold and/or silver, but by the blood of Jesus, who paid it as price for our salvation.

CHAPTER 13
STORMS CALMED DOWN

"But the men marvelled, saying, What manner of man is this, that even the winds and the sea obey him!" (Matthew 8:27)

There was great multitude of people following Jesus as they saw the miracles done by Him. They saw how a leper was healed; they saw how centurion's servant was healed and they also saw Peter's mother-in-law was healed.

When Jesus touched Peter's mother-in-law, who was suffering from fever, He was not trying to diagnose her disease, nor was He trying to console her but His touching was a powerful healing-touch that healed her fully. There was no trace of fatigue left in her nor was she feeling tired anymore but she rose up and ministered unto them.

Jesus looked at the crowd that expected more miracles from Him and said to them to go to the other side of the sea, which was "Sea of Galilee". Just before leaving to the other side of the sea He had conversation with a scribe who expressed his desire to follow Him but Jesus showed him how hard it was to follow Him.

When Jesus spoke to another he expressed his difficulty in following Him but Jesus said to him to follow Him. He said that those who are spiritually dead may go and attend to their earthly needs. Thus two different types of men were introduced to us; one that half-heartedly expressing his desire to follow Jesus and another with full of excuses when the Lord asked him to follow.

As Jesus entered the ship to go to the other side His disciples followed Him. His sailing by the sea helped future generations to have hope in the Lord that He helps those that seek His help. Jesus chose to go by sea-way instead of going by the road-way in order that His journey by the sea would be of much comfort to those who usually undertake travel by sea. It was going to be a sure sign for future sailors that they can pray to Him for their safe journey and seek His help.

Jesus was taking rest just as any human would do after tiresome job. Jesus, the Son of God, taking rest shows us that He was fully human when He was in this world. He was tired and was sleeping but He was not as deep in His sleep as Jonah was, many years ago, in the ship while trying to escape to a possible secure place from the task he was assigned. In Jesus we have our salvation and He is our redeemer.

As they were journeying there arose a vigorous tempest in the sea so much that the waves from the sea covered the ship. Indeed, everyone in the ship, except Jesus, was afraid of the tempest. Their nerves started shrinking as they saw the tempest even when the creator of the seas was right there in their midst. How often we also fear, in spite of having faith in Jesus, that some misadventure would overtake us.

The Lord would have to remind us through some servant of God or through His word that He is always there with us. Indeed, He is our comfort and sustainer. It is worth recollecting Psalmist's comforting words.

"O love the LORD, all ye his saints: for the LORD preserveth the faithful, and plentifully rewardeth the proud doer. Be of good courage, and he shall strengthen your heart, all ye that hope in the LORD" (Psalms 31:23-24)

Jesus could have ordered the sea to be calm even before they started their journey or when they were sailing but He preferred not to do so and He showed that He was in control of the situation, over waters and the storms in order that His disciples may become stronger in their faith in Him. When the severity of the storm increased the disciples were afraid. The disciples went to Lord Jesus, who was sleeping in the same ship, and awoke Him. They begged saying "Lord, save us: we perish". They were praying for not only themselves but on behalf of all the sailors who were in the ship. They thought the storms would drown the ship. However, they realized that the Lord of the sea was in ship, and He would be able to save them. Therefore, they prayed to Jesus to save them and Jesus heard their prayer.

Jesus admonished them that they were fearful because they lacked faith. Then He arose and rebuked the winds and sea and there was great calm. The men in the ship marveled at the miracle and wondered about the power that Jesus exercised on storms and on the winds that they obeyed His command.

Indeed Lord Jesus Christ is the Savior. Much more than the comfort that we have that our Lord has the power over storms we cast our burden on Him and rest in His arms because He gave us salvation free of cost. While those whose sins are not forgiven and do not have Lord Jesus Christ as their savior would have to gnash their teeth in the "Lake of fire", where fire never quenches, we will be with Him for ever and ever.

"And he saith unto them, Why are ye fearful, O ye of little faith? Then he arose, and rebuked the winds and the sea; and there was a great calm" (Matthew 8:26

)

CHAPTER 14
PETER AND JOHN

"While he yet spake, behold, a bright cloud overshadowed them: and behold a voice out of the cloud, which said, This is my beloved Son, in whom I am well pleased; hear ye him." (Matthew 17:5)

Peter and also the two sons of Zebedee (James and John) saw Jesus transfigured and his face shone as the sun, and his raiment was white as light, when he appeared to them. They also heard the Father saying"... This is my beloved Son, in whom I am well pleased; hear ye him..." (Matthew 17:5).

Peter was perturbed on hearing false stories about Jesus and about the unbelief about Jesus. Therefore, he testified that he and James and John witnessed the event of transfiguration of Jesus. Peter said that they did not follow cunning devised fables about Jesus; but they made known about Jesus and his glory to them as eye witnesses. Peter testified that they made known unto them the power and coming of Lord Jesus Christ.

They said that they were eye witnesses of his majesty and that they heard the voice that came down from heaven, while they were on the holy mountain. (2 Peter 1:16-18) Peter heard Jesus say that the Father loves him because he lays down his life and will take it again. (John 10:17).

John testified that "the Word was made flesh, and dwelt among us, (and we beheld his glory, the glory as of the only begotten of the Father,) full of grace and truth". (John 1:14)

True, we enjoy the benefits of the love of God because Jesus laid down his life our sake; "But God raised him from the dead" (Acts 13:30). We are cleansed of our sins by the blood of Jesus Christ shed on the cross. This is the truth and faith in him alone saves a person from damnation.

Do not trust every spirit, but test the sprits to know for yourself whether or not those spirits are of God. There are many false prophets and preachers gone out into this world.

The way to know whether someone is from the living God or not is to make sure whether or not that person confesses that Jesus Christ is the incarnation of the Father and dwelt among us.

Anyone, who does not confess that Jesus is come in the flesh, is not of God but of antichrist. There are many out there now who say that a man can gain salvation by good works. It is time we know them and realize that they are not from God.

If you are not yet saved, here is word from Apostle Paul, who says that if you confess with your mouth the Lord Jesus and believe in your heart that God raised him from the dead you shall be saved. (Romans 10:9)

CHAPTER 15
LITTLE LOWER THAN ANGELS

Let us ponder on the creation account mentioned in Genesis Chapter 1. God made heavens, earth, plants, and animals by His word and command, but when it came to make man God took some time to make him in his own image. I was thinking that God may have taken quite a great deal of delight to see tiny flies move around, tiny birds jump around, animals jump around, lions roaring, and elephants moving around.

After creating man God desired to have fellowship with him and loved him so much. He gave him a helpmate and the man called her as Woman.

The Woman was called as "Eve" because she was the mother of all living. The man was called as "Adam" (Gen. 2:19). The Woman was called as "Eve" (Gen 3:20).

When we create some art-work or draw a picture we are delighted to see our work and appreciate it. We want others to appreciate our work and appreciate us for doing that work. Let us think how much God desires to see we appreciate his work, his wisdom, and his ability to create the universe, the earth, the galaxy, the seas, you and me.

God also created supernatural heavenly beings that are called as Angels. The word in Hebrew and Greek from which the word "Angels" derived was also applied to human messengers. It is recorded in Colossians 1:16 that all things whether visible or invisible were created by God and for him. In Hebrews 1:4-8 it is recorded that the Son of God, Lord Jesus Christ was greater than angels. The Father said "Thou art my Son, this day I have begotten thee" and He has ordered the entire angelic host to worship the Son of God.

The Father also said to him that his throne is for and ever and the scepter of righteousness is the scepter of his kingdom.

Yet when Jesus was in the form of man on this earth he was considered as little lower than the angels, just as man was considered as lower than the angels. Man is given the glory and honor to have dominion over all the works of God.

The angels are the ministering spirits created by God. He takes care of the children of God. Jesus is always with the saved ones, and many times the children of God see angels helping children of God. Think about the wonderful way God has exalted man.

The words of Psalmist as prophesied in Psalm 8:3-9 are repeated in Hebrews 2:6-8 as fulfillment of the prophesy.

"When I consider thy heavens, the work of thy fingers, the moon and the stars, which thou hast ordained; What is man, that thou art mindful of him? and the son of man, that thou visitest him? For thou hast made him a little lower than the angels, and hast crowned him with glory and honour.

Thou madest him to have dominion over the works of thy hands; thou hast put all things under his feet: All sheep and oxen, yea, and the beasts of the field" (Psalms 8:3-7)

And, in Hebrews 2:9 we have wonderful declaration that Jesus was made little lower than angels for suffering death on behalf of us and was crowned with glory and honor.

But we see Jesus, who was made a little lower than the angels for the suffering of death, crowned with glory and honour; that he by the grace of God should taste death for every man. (Hebrews 2:9)

CHAPTER 16
PUT ON THE ARMOUR OF GOD

"Put on the whole armour of God, that ye may be able to stand against the wiles of the devil". (Ephesians 6:11)

In the battle that was to take place between the army of Philistines and the army of children of Israel both were advantageously posted, yet neither went forward to fight against each other.

Philistine hero Goliath was waiting for an equivalent opponent. Saul thought there was none on his side to fight against this mighty proud warrior.

David the youngest son of Jesse, looking after his father's sheep, went to watch as to what was happening in the battlefield. To his surprise, he found that none from the Israelites' camp went forward to fight against Goliath.

Deeply distressed over the attitude of his brothers and also that of others in the camp, he agreed to fight with Goliath. David retorted and said "who is this uncircumcised fellow to mock at God's children?" David took the challenge and went forward to face Goliath.

Seeing the shepherd boy the giant Goliath insulted him. David was a shepherd boy, short in stature and did not attire himself in good dress. Saul was worried about the intervention of this shepherd boy, David. "And Saul said to David, Thou art not able to go against this Philistine to fight with him: for thou art but a youth, and he a man of war from his youth". (1 Samuel 17:33) What a discouragement David had to face from Saul!

Yet after hearing David's courageous acts Saul conceded to David to fight against the Philistine but asked David to wear "his armour, and he put on helmet of brass upon his head and also armed him with a coat of mail". (1 Samuel 17:38).

Saul thought armor, helmet of brass and coat are required to meet challenge of enemy. He insisted upon David to wear armor of his choice to face Goliath. Saul himself did not have courage to face Goliath but he thought David needed his choice armor to face the enemy. David girded his sword upon his armour and found uncomfortable. He removed it saying that he cannot go with the armour that Saul has provided him. (1 Samuel 17:39)

David took his staff and chose five smooth stones out of the brook and he hurled a stone from his sling. The stone sunk into Goliath's forehead and he fell upon his face to the earth. (1 Samuel 17:40 and 49)

David ran and stood upon Philistine and took his sword and killed him and the philistines fled from the battlefield (1 Samuel 17:50-51)

David used Goliath's own weapon to kill him. God was with David. Goliath's strength and power were of no avail before God's.

The same God, the living Lord, who has sent His Son, Jesus Christ, into this world for the remission of your sins and mine, calls us to depend on Him because He is our savior. He wants to be our rock of refuge and bless us. He wants us to put on the armor that he gave us instead of putting on the armor that the world gives us. Let not the strong man glory in his strength.

CHAPTER 17
STREET OF GOLD

"And the twelve gates were twelve pearls; every several gate was of one pearl: and the street of the city was pure gold, as it were transparent glass". (Revelation 21:21)

In this secular world we see the importance of gold. What if we who are common people in this world can tread on a street of gold, and live in a city made of the most precious metals?

Bible speaks of such precious metals, which even common man tread on, and live in a city made of most precious metals. Revelation chapter 21 presents the most beautiful city and the inhabitants there in.

John saw in his vision the holy city, New Jerusalem, coming down out of heaven from God, prepared for a bride, who was adorned for her husband. The description is great. Who is this bride? Bible speaks of the bride as the Church/Assembly constituting the believers in Christ, the saved ones.

The bride is adorned waiting for her husband to come and here is the chaste virgin, adorned waiting for the New Jerusalem.

The tabernacle is referred to in the Old Testament, as the sacred tent in which God came and dwelt. Here in this chapter John saw God himself coming down and dwelling among his people, who will be his people, and he will be their God, who will wipe away all their tears, and there will be no more death, nor sorrow, nor crying, no more pain, because all the old things have passed away by then.

It is the new heaven where the Assembly/Church, constituting the saved ones, which is his bride, will dwell.

Isaiah 65:17 presents the prophecy about the new heavens and a new earth that will be created and about the former earth and heaven which will pass away and will not be remembered.

In Revelation 21:1 we read that city, which is beautiful and which has no sea, but only the inhabitants, who are always happy and without any sufferings. . Rev 21: 18 "And the building of the wall of it was of jasper: and the city was pure gold, like unto clear glass"

 Our savior Jesus Christ has undergone severe pain when men pierced sword in to his body and beat him. He was crowned with a crown of thorns and blood and water gushed forth from the side of his body.

It is through that blood of Jesus Christ that we are saved. He suffered on the cross of Calvary that so that we may have eternal life. It is through the shedding of his precious blood that our sins are cleansed and through that blood of Christ that our filth is cleansed and we are made clear as crystal. That city of precious metals is prepared for us."

But for those who do not accept Jesus Christ as their personal Savior, there is another place designated and it is the lake of fire, as we read in Rev. 21: 8. It is described as the "lake which burneth with fire and brimstone" which is the second death.

And I saw no temple in it: for the Lord God Almighty and the Lamb are the temple of it. And the city had no need of the sun, neither of the moon, to shine in it: for the glory of God is its light, and the Lamb is its lamp. (Revelation 21:22-23)

CHAPTER 18
ANTICHRIST

There is a description of Antichrist in Revelation Chapter 13. This Antichrist is not revealed to the world until the Church is taken away by the Lord and Holy Spirit is withdrawn from this world.

Antichrist promises peace in the world and makes many other promises to please men. At the end of his three and half years of rule he breaks all the promises that he made and brings in hardships on the people. These hardships are the 'great tribulation'. This will last for three and half years and his regime ends.

Jesus warns in Matthew 24:4-7 about Antichrist and he instructs his disciples to be careful about the false prophets, false teachers, and also asks that they need to pray that their flight may not be in winter. He instructed them that they would hear of wars, rumors of wars, but all those things must come to pass, but still the end is not yet. Lord Jesus told them in John 16:33 that he spoke unto them these things, so that they may have peace, because in this world they would have tribulation.

These tribulations are not similar to the 'great tribulation' that the Jews and the left-behind will face during the Antichrist regime. These tribulations are the ones, which every Christian will face in his/her life, when he/she is in this world. Jesus asks all of us to be comfortable because Jesus had overcome the world and he had successfully faced these kinds of tribulations on this earth.

The 'great tribulation' is different from the usual tribulations we face in our lives. Great tribulation is universal; it is not limited to a local place. It is as the world has never seen before. It would be more severe than the one that had passed by in AD 70, when many Jews were crucified upside down on the walls of Jerusalem.

"Beloved, believe not every spirit, but try the spirits whether they are of God: because many false prophets are gone out into the world. Hereby know ye the Spirit of God: Every spirit that confesseth that Jesus Christ is come in the flesh is of God: And every spirit that confesseth not that Jesus Christ is come in the flesh is not of God: and this is that spirit of antichrist, whereof ye have heard that it should come; and even now already is it in the world". (1 John 4:1-3)

John wrote about those who oppose Christ, but the description given in Revelation Chapter 13 is of the one who tries to take the position of Christ. That is of the one who would try himself to substitute in the place of Lord Jesus Christ.

For those who are left behind this 'man of sin', also known as the 'son of perdition' will appear, and he will rule over them. This Antichrist is worshipped by all those who are loyal to him and also by those who cannot tolerate the 'Great Tribulation' during that period. His number is "666".

Antichrist forces his dictatorship to such an extent that no one can sell or buy anything unless he has a mark on his right hand or on his forehead this mark of the beast.

This is one world economy. But then, there will be those who disobey him and call upon the Lord to save them. Jews will call upon the Lord to save them and the Lord helps them. These are those who are saved during great tribulation period, but they are not part of the Church and they will not have the blessings of the Church.

"Here is wisdom. Let him that hath understanding count the number of the beast: for it is the number of a man; and his number is Six hundred threescore and six". Revelation 13:18)

There are those who say that they do not worship any god but they will worship this beast the 'man of sin' who is also known as 'the son of perdition'. What a shame that atheists who say that they do not have god and do not worship anyone, but will worship this man, and consider him as God.

There have been some shadows of this kind in the form of some religious leaders, whom people worshipped; but the real religious leader under one government in the world is yet to come. And that man cannot be seen by the Church because before his appearance the Church would have been 'caught up' into the mid-air to be with the Lord for ever and ever.

The Church is the precious bride of Lord Jesus Christ and we, who are the members of the Church, will not have to see this Antichrist. Thanks to God. Note here when

Antichrist and false prophet are thrown into the lake of fire! It is before the devil that deceived!!!

Does the Scripture say anybody is thrown into the lake of fire before Antichrist and false prophet? No, not at all!

At the end of the seven-year period Lord Jesus Christ with his bride, which is the Church, descends and steps on the Mount of Olives. Then follows sheep and Goat Judgment; one-thousand-year-reign of Jesus Christ; Satan being released from abyss; Satan going Gog and Magog to gather from the nations armies for himself to fight against Jesus; fire from heaven coming down and defeating Satan and his fallen angels; the resurrection of the unsaved; great white throne judgment; and casting off death, hell, Satan and his fallen angels, and all those who have not accepted Jesus as their savior into the 'lake of fire'.

"And the devil that deceived them was cast into the lake of fire and brimstone, where the beast and the false prophet are, and shall be tormented day and night for ever and ever" (Revelation 20:10).

Notice that when the devil was cast into the lake of fire, the Antichrist and the false prophet were already there in the lake of fire. These are only the ones who will be in the lake of fire before the 'Great White Throne Judgment' (Revelation 16:16 and Revelation 20:8-10)

THE JUDGMENT OF THE WICKED

And I saw a great white throne, and him that sat on it, from whose face the earth and the heaven fled away;

and there was found no place for them. And I saw the dead, small and great, stand before God; and the books were opened: and another book was opened, which is the book of life: and the dead were judged out of those things which were written in the books, according to their works. (Revelation 20:11 -12)

This is the 'Great White Throne judgment', which is the final judgment, where everyone, whose name is not found in the book of life is judged and 'death and hell will be cast into the lake of fire. This is the second death'. (Rev. 20:14)

CHPTER 19
THE THOUSAND YEAR REIGN

God promised Abraham that in Isaac will be the blessed people who will be His people and He will be their God. Jesus came to save the children of Israel, yet they rejected him. This paved the way for Gentiles to come to him for salvation and secure God's mercy.

All those who had believed Jesus as their savior and laid faith in him were saved and all those who believe in him shall be saved. Two thieves were crucified on either side of Lord Jesus. One of them mocked Jesus while the other sought mercy from Jesus. He prayed that Jesus may remember him when He comes in his Kingdom.

Jesus said to the thief who prayed for mercy that he would be in Paradise the very same day as Jesus died. Jesus was buried and rose from the dead on the third, ascended into heaven and is seated on the right hand of the Majesty. He would come soon. Salvation is available to anyone who calls upon Jesus for mercy.

Isaiah 40:11 says "He shall feed his flock like a shepherd: he shall gather the lambs with his arm, and carry [them] in his bosom, [and] shall gently lead those that are with young"

Israel has become one nation in 1948 but they do not have the shepherd yet. They rejected Jesus as their Messiah and called for his blood to be upon them. Has

God forgotten Israel because they rejected him as their Messiah? No. God said "Can a woman forget her sucking child, that she should not have compassion on the son of her womb? yea, they may forget, yet will I not forget thee". Isaiah 49:15

The things are going to be worse for them that they will call for help from Jesus. He would not come until they realize that they have rejected him and they need him. They will face terrible persecution under Antichrist in the last days.

They would cry that the mountains may fall on them and kill them (Rev.6:16). Israel will call upon God during the Great Tribulation period. God is not going to leave them but he will bring them on their knees to call upon his help. Then shall the Lord come to them and be their King of kings and Lord of lords. Jesus will literally reign for thousand years sitting on the throne of David.

John saw in his vision those who were martyrs for Jesus and for the word of God and also those who did not worship the Antichrist in the thousand year reign.

 Those that did not believe on Jesus did not rise from their graves. They will be thrown into the lake of fire. But, all those whose sins are washed in the blood of Jesus, irrespective of Jews or Gentiles will be caught up together to meet the Lord in the air even before the Great Tribulation starts and will be with the Lord for ever.

The dead shall rise first and we who are alive and remain shall be caught up together with them in the clouds to meet the Lord in the air: and so shall be ever be with the Lord. (1 Thessalonians 4:16-17)

"And I saw thrones, and they sat upon them, and judgment was given unto them: and [I saw] the souls of them that were beheaded for the witness of Jesus, and for the word of God, and which had not worshipped the beast, neither his image, neither had received [his] mark upon their foreheads, or in their hands; and they lived and reigned with Christ a thousand years" Revelation 20:4"

CHAPTER 20
REFUGE IN THE LIVING GOD

This meditation is about two individuals in the war between Philistines and the children of Israel at a land that belonged to Judah. The first one was Goliath, who was proud, huge, tall, strong man from Philistines. The second one was David, the son of Jesse, who belonged to the children of Israel.

Philistines took pride in their leader Goliath in the battle at Shochloh, which belonged to Judah. Saul and men of Israel gathered on the other side by the valley of Elah. Philistines stood on a mountain on one side and the Israel stood on a mountain on the other side (1 Samuel 17:1-3)

Saul was the first king of Israel. He was the son of Kish from the tribe of Benjamin. He was young, handsome and taller than anyone among the children of Israel. (1 Samuel 9:1-2)

There was no response to Goliath's challenge either from Saul or anyone from Israel until the ruddy shepherd David came along to take up the challenge. Goliath looked upon David with scorn and shouted.

Goliath ridiculed the God of Israel and wondered if David thought that Goliath was a dog! He boasted in his gods and said that he would give David's flesh to the fowls of the air and to the beasts of the field.

The response from David who hoped in the Almighty and living God was equally challenging. David honored the living God when he said to Goliath that he was facing the mighty man in the name of the Lord of hosts, the God of armies of Israel, whom Goliath defied.

"Then said David to the Philistine, Thou comest to me with a sword, and with a spear, and with a shield: but I come to thee in the name of the LORD of hosts, the God of the armies of Israel, whom thou hast defied.

This day will the LORD deliver thee into mine hand; and I will smite thee, and take thine head from thee; and I will give the carcases of the host of the Philistines this day unto the fowls of the air, and to the wild beasts of the earth; that all the earth may know that there is a God in Israel". (1 Samuel 17:45-46)

Goliath arose, went to meet David in the battlefield, and drew close, like a stalking mountain, overlaid with brass and iron.

David advanced with greater strength in God and cheerfulness, as one that aimed more to execute God's command rather than to make a figure: He hasted, and ran, was being lightly clad, to meet the Philistine. Before honor is humility.

David put one of the pebbles in the sling and hurled at Goliath. There it was! The pebble struck straight at Goliath's forehead and in the twinkling of an eye, it fetched him to the ground. Goliath fell with his face down on the ground.

"Therefore David ran, and stood upon the Philistine, and took his sword, and drew it out of the sheath thereof, and slew him, and cut off his head therewith. And when the Philistines saw their champion was dead, they fled". (1 Samuel 17:51)

CHAPTER 21
TRUST IN THE LORD

Jesus walked on water. Peter was about to sink because he feared the tumultuous wind. As long as Peter looked unto Jesus he was able to walk on the water just as Jesus himself was walking on the water, but when Peter feared seeing the wind boisterous he started sinking. Peter, then, called upon his savior to save him.

Jesus immediately stretched forth his hand and lifted Peter from sinking.

"But when he saw the wind boisterous, he was afraid; and beginning to sink, he cried, saying, Lord, save me. And immediately Jesus stretched forth his hand, and caught him, and said unto him, O thou of little faith, wherefore didst thou doubt? " Matthew 14:30-31

Jesus sent away multitudes of men, woman and children, whom he fed with five loaves and two fishes, and moved into a desert place.

This was after he heard that John was beheaded. Jesus asked his disciples to go by ship to the other side of the sea and he went up into a mountain to pray until the evening. He was all alone there but the ship was in the midst of the sea and the strong winds blew and sea tossed with waves. Jesus went toward the ship in the night.

The disciples saw Jesus walking on the water and coming toward them, but they feared that it was a spirit and cried. It was then that Jesus their savior told them to be of good cheer and said it was he, who was walking toward them. Peter was eager to walk on water.

Peter asked Jesus if Jesus could call him to walk on water toward him. When Peter sought help to go near to him Jesus said to him 'come down out the ship '.

As Peter was making endeavors to walk toward Jesus he saw that the wind was boisterous, and got frightened. As soon as Peter got frightened he started sinking and cried to Jesus saying "Lord, save me".

Jesus did not leave Peter helpless, but immediately stretched forth his hand and caught him. Jesus admonished Peter of his little faith. Seeing that Peter was failing Jesus questioned him as to why he doubted.

Peter's doubt and fear brought failure to himself, but as soon as he called out for help from Jesus he readily helped Peter. When they came into the ship the wind stopped. Then all those who were in the ship came and worshipped him, saying that Jesus was the Son of God.

Doubt causes fear resulting in loss of faith and yet when calling on God will bring success. Give God a chance to work in you, rather than having alternate plans to work for yourself with your own wisdom and strength.

Psalmist says - "Some trust in chariots, and some in horses: but we will remember the name of the LORD our God." (Psalms 20:7)"

"And we know that all things work together for good to them that love God, to them who are the called according to his purpose". (Romans 8:28)

The children of Israel had reached the borders of the Promised Land and it would not take many days to get into the land. But at that time the LORD spoke to Moses saying that he should send men one from each tribe of their fathers to the Promised land of Canaan and spy out the land and see if the people living there were strong or weak, few or many, whether the land was good or bad, whether the cities they live in were tents or strong holds, whether or not the land was rich or poor, whether or not there was wood and then commanded them to be of good courage and bring of the fruit of the land. He also suggested that the grapes were ripe then. (Numbers 13:1-2, Numbers 13:17-20)

A quick reading of this chapter will surely render misunderstanding that it was God's plan to send the spies to the land of Canaan and check it out whether the land of Canaan was really good or not. But it was not so. God did not need to check the strength of the men who were living in Canaan.

God knew that the land which He promised to the children of Israel was very good one and it was a land where milk and honey was flowing. The land was rich in fruit, wood and cities were strong.

God promised the best for the children of Israel and there was no need for Him to send spies to search the land that He may change His promise. No, it was not so. It was the request of the children of Israel that the LORD was responding to. God had already promised the

Israelites that the land of Canaan was given to them for their possession. All that they had to do was to believe on the LORD and go forward to possess it.

"Behold, the LORD thy God hath set the land before thee: go up and possess it, as the LORD God of thy fathers hath said unto thee; fear not, neither be discouraged". (Deuteronomy 1:21)

But the children of Israel had been murmuring from the time they left Egypt until they reached the borders of the Promised Land.

They were at Kadeshbarnea, which was very close to the Promised Land of Canaan (Deuteronomy 1:19); but then it was they who decided that they would send spies to search the land and bring them report. That is to say that they did not depend on God's word but wanted to depend on the report which their own men would present to them and consider whether or not they should enter the Promised Land of Canaan.

Israelites murmured against Moses and the LORD and felt that their journey in the wilderness was not worth leaving the land of Egypt (Deuteronomy 1:22-27) Thus they displeased the LORD many a time on their journey. Their mindset was still of slavery even when they were at the borders of the land of Canaan.

They did not trust the LORD in spite of seeing miraculous protection they had all through their journey; they never lacked food or water, yet they murmured against the LORD and worshipped idols on their journey from Egypt to Canaan.

"And ye murmured in your tents, and said, Because the LORD hated us, he hath brought us forth out of the land of Egypt, to deliver us into the hand of the Amorites, to destroy us". (Deuteronomy 1:27)

Hebrews 11:1 says: "Now faith is the substance of things hoped for, the evidence of things not seen".

Here in this particular situation we see that the children of Israel failed in faith and tempted God. They did not trust that God, who promised them the land of Canaan, would be really the God worth believing.

They did not believe that the land of Canaan was really the land where milk and honey was flowing. God gave them the promise that this rich land will be given to them for their possession. It was given even when they were still under the bondage of slavery (Exodus 3:8).

God delivered them from the bondage under Pharaoh and led them through the wilderness unto the borders of Canaan, where they stopped to murmur again losing their faith in God.

It was as if they would decide for themselves whether or not they want to enter the land of Canaan. The promise was about to be fulfilled when the children of Israel had doubted God's promise and reaped the consequences.

Once again, God agreed to their request and said to Moses that he should send twelve men one from each of the tribe of their fathers to spy out and bring the news.

The LORD agreed that they may really see if God's word was right. Moses sent twelve men as commanded. As we read further in Numbers Chapters 13 and 14 we see that the children of Israel paid the price for their unbelief and rebellion against the LORD.

Let us trust God that He will always do well to us.

"There is therefore now no condemnation to them which are in Christ Jesus, who walk not after the flesh, but after the Spirit". (Romans 8:1)

"Behold, the LORD thy God hath set the land before thee: go up [and] possess [it], as the LORD God of thy fathers hath said unto thee; fear not, neither be discouraged" Deuteronomy 1:21

The twelve men chosen as spies to spy out the land of Canaan searched the land and returned to their camp after forty days. Except Joshua, the son of Nun and Caleb, the son of Jephunneh, the other ten men gave report and suggested not to enter the land of Canaan.

Every one of the twelve gave report but the ten men (other than Joshua and Caleb) gave a report filled with disbelief, cowardice and fear. They showed the fruit of the land, especially a branch with one cluster of grapes, which was carried by two of them on a staff, and of pomegranates and of the figs.

Anyone who saw vineyard would know that a cluster of grapes on branch does not require two men to carry it on a staff, but the cluster of grapes that they picked up from the brook of Eshcol in the land of Canaan was so big that it needed two men to carry it on a staff.

Indeed, this shows that the land was plenteous in good fruit.

This was the land that God promised to the children of Israel. (Numbers 13:23-24)

The ten men who gave evil report of the land of Canaan said to Moses that the land was indeed very good and it surely flowed with milk and honey but the men, who were living there were giants and strong.

The report was filled with facts about the abundance and those facts were true. The report was corroborating with God's assurance of the abundance in that land. God told them about it even when they were still under the bondage in Egypt. The facts about the land that their report presented did not change the truth that God told them earlier.

God knew it earlier and promised the land to them for their possession. But as they came to the borders of the land of Promised land they doubted and wanted to spy out the land and have conviction that God's saying was really so. What a disbelief they had!

It was God who promised the land with milk and honey flowing but they chose to confirm if the truth that God said to them was really so. They trusted in their own strength and wisdom rather than God's promise.

The ten men not only presented an evil report but presented along with the report great discouragement, and fear. As they were journeying in the wilderness for forty years they saw God's power in defeating their enemies, yet, when they saw giants in the land of Canaan they were afraid.

They saw the children of Anak, Amalekites on the south, Hittites, Jebusites, and Amorites in the mountain region and Canaanites by the sea and by the cost of Jordan. They said that they felt like grasshoppers before those giants and, therefore, suggested to Moses that the children of Israel should not venture entering the land of Canaan. They have put all their efforts of their travel from Egypt to the borders of Canaan into the purview of pessimism.

Israelites lost faith in God and trusted in their own strength. Whereas the giants would have been made like grasshoppers before the children of Israel if they truly depended on God, now the giants in their sight appeared huge.

They felt that they were like grasshoppers before the giants. Fear brings disappointment and loss of faith in the one who promised better things. They lost faith in the strength of the Almighty and feared them because they were huge. (Numbers 13:33)

Nevertheless, Caleb and Joshua were not of that spirit of cowardice, but of full of faith and courage. They spoke to Moses and encouraged him to go forward to possess the land that flowed with milk and honey. They saw the fruit of the land that it was good and the huge physical structure of the giants of that land did not bring disappointment or fear in them. Caleb said "Let us go up at once, and possess it, for we are well able to overcome it" (Numbers 13:30).

As we read Numbers Chapter 14 we see that the children of Israel stoned Moses and wanted to go back to Egypt from where they came. Moses was protected by divine power and no danger came upon him but ponder over the rebellion in the minds of the children of Israel. They decided to choose another captain for them and return to the land of Egypt where they served as slaves.

Israelites were freed by God, yet they were trying to choose to return to that slavery. They saw the mighty power of God, wonderful protection of God and they had sumptuous food and sweet water on their journey. They had the presence of God with them when He came down and dwelt among them in the Tabernacle, yet they were afraid when they saw the giants.

This is the condition of many believers even now. Fear encompasses their minds resulting in loss of faith and increase in disappointment. But God wants us not to return to the slavery under sin but be of good courage and fruitful to him.

God blesses those who rejoice in Him. God is loving and long-suffering. Jesus is standing at the door of your heart and knocking at your door. If you will, He will enter in and dwell there. There are number of references in the New Testament for believers in Christ to have faith in Jesus that they may live a life of sufficiency, and of peace without any fear.

In Matthew 6:30 Jesus asks if God can clothe the grass of the field that does not live long how much more God can clothe the believers who depend on him. That was an assurance from him that the believers in him do not need to worry as to how they would be clothed, but seek the kingdom of God first.

In Matthew 8:10 Jesus marveled at the faith of a Gentile Centurion who believed in Jesus and sought that his servant who lay with sick of palsy and grievously tormented may be healed. Jesus marveled that even in Israel he did not see such great faith and said to the Centurion "Go thy way; and as thou hast believed, so be it done unto thee. And his servant was healed in the selfsame hour" (Matthew 8:13)

In Matthew 8:26 we see that the disciples of Jesus were afraid when they saw the tempest in the sea while they were sailing in a ship. They prayed to Jesus to save them that they may not perish.

Jesus wondered at their lack of faith and asked them as to why they were fearful, and called them "O ye of little faith", and then he arose and rebuked the winds and the sea. The winds and the sea obeyed him and the sea calmed down. The men marveled that even the winds and the sea obey Jesus.

The same Jesus is asking us to trust him that he may be with us always and help us. If we trust him he will give us peace not as the world gives, but He gives us His peace.

"Peace I leave with you, my peace I give unto you: not as the world giveth, give I unto you. Let not your heart be troubled, neither let it be afraid" John 14:27.

CHAPTER 22
DO NOT FEAR GIANTS

"But the very hairs of your head are all numbered"
(Matthew 10:30)

Is it not wonderful that our God knows us not only by
our names but by every detail that is in us including the
number of hairs on our head. He has count of them and
yet we stumble in faith several times. It is our weakness
that we fail to understand the mighty power of God and
his provision for us.

However, we should be aware of the fact that if we
neglect or doubt his care for us we will reap the
consequences of our disbelief and run into loss.

The children of Israel stumbled upon their faith in the
Lord and paid severely for their lack of faith. They
feared that the giants whom their representatives saw
were capable of harming them whereas God said no
weapon formed against them will prosper.

Every one of the age above twenty years including
Moses and Aaron, except Joshua and Caleb, died before
they reached the Promised Land of Canaan. The details
are in Numbers chapter 14

On hearing the evil report from the ten spies the
congregation cried whole night and murmured against
Moses and Aaron. The congregation asked Moses and
Aaron if God wanted them to die in the wilderness and
asked why they were moved out of Egypt with the

promise that they would have a better life! Then after hearing the evil report from the ten they preferred to go back to slavery in Egypt rather than die in the wilderness. This was their disappointment because of their lack of faith in God who promised them the land flowing with milk and honey.

This was the result of their lack of belief in God who gave them protection from rain and heat. They never lacked food, nor did their shoe wear out during their entire journey for forty years. But they believed the discouraging evil report of the ten men who went out to make a survey of the land.

They sent their emissaries to make their own choice despite God's promise that he would bless them with land that had abundance. Their own witnesses brought a cluster of grapes hanging on a staff carried by two men from that land to them to see, yet when they heard that there were Anakites, who were giants they lost faith.

Perhaps, they thought their God was smaller than the giants their men saw in the land. The men felt that they were like grasshoppers before the giants in spite of the fact that they defeated mighty kings on their journey with the help of God.

Now that the children of Israelites were entrapped in their own false beliefs and lack of faith in God, they forged forward to kill Moses and Aaron, who were interceding on behalf of them to God all through their journey.

The children of Israel were making a decision to choose a captain to lead them back to Egypt from where they came to Kadeshbarnea, which was so close to the Promised Land. They wanted to go back from blessings to curse and lead a life of slavery in a sinful land once again. Earlier, when they were in Egypt crying to God for help and prayed that they may be delivered from the slavery, God heard their cry and redeemed them from the bondage of slavery under Pharaoh.

Until God executed the last plague of killing the firstborn of Egyptians, Pharaoh did not allow them to leave Egypt.

Israelites saw that their own firstborn were spared by God, yet now listening to disappointing evil report they changed their mind. How feeble and frail was their mind that they lost faith in their God and believed in the evil report.

Moses, who interceded on their behalf several times, fell once again face down before the congregation of all the children of Israel to cry to the Lord. Aaron accompanied Moses in his prayers and Joshua and Caleb tore down their clothes to support Moses and Aaron.

God heard their prayer and promised them pardon yet their earthly blessings of possessing the land of Canaan were lost to them in their time. That land which was with milk and honey flowing was promised to them for their possession but all those who started their journey from Egypt, except Joshua and Caleb and those who were below the age of twenty years, perished in the wilderness.

If you are not yet saved this is the day for accepting Jesus as your personal savior. Do not fear any adversity. You are of more value than many sparrows, who toil not, yet they have their food and protection every day. If you are saved already, then never fear those who have the authority over your flesh but fear the one who has the authority over body, soul and spirit. Jesus said he has overcome this world. He is Lord Jesus Christ who is the only savior. Salvation of a believer is never lost, yet believer should live a holy life always.

"Fear ye not therefore, ye are of more value than many sparrows. Whosoever therefore shall confess me before men, him will I confess also before my Father which is in heaven" (Matthew 10:31-32)

CHAPTER 23
TRUST GOOD REPORT

"Finally, brethren, whatsoever things are true, whatsoever things are honest, whatsoever things are just, whatsoever things are pure, whatsoever things are lovely, whatsoever things are of good report; if there be any virtue, and if there be any praise, think on these things". (Philippians 4:8)

Apostle Paul writes in his epistle to Philippians that they should rejoice in the Lord, and not be worried of anything; rather submit their prayers and supplications to God. He also advises that whatsoever things are true, honest, pure, and lovely and whatsoever are of good report and if there is any virtue in them, then they should consider them as acceptable.

Of the twelve men who went to spy the land of Canaan and bring report of it, ten brought a report that presented a true picture of the abundance in the land, yet they were afraid of the giants.

Even though their report was true of the abundance of the land yet their report of the men in that land was evil. They presented a very poor picture of their own strength against the giants they saw in the land of Canaan.

They forgot that God's strength was always there with them and yet they were afraid of the giants in the Promised Land.

Of the twelve men who went to spy the land of Canaan and bring report of it, two brought a report that presented not only a true picture of the abundance of that land but they gave an excellent report of their own strength in the Lord and faith that they can defeat the giants in the land of Canaan.

The two men who presented a good report were Joshua, the son of Nun and Caleb, the son of Jephunneh.

Joshua and Caleb gave an encouraging and a true report to Moses and Aaron and all the congregation of the Israel, of the land of Canaan and said that the land that they saw was exceedingly good.

Their faith was in the living God and said if God was pleased he would give the land to them. They requested that the congregation be patient and not rebel against their leaders. They said to the people that there is no need to be afraid of the giants in the land of Canaan that all the twelve men saw.

They gave assurance that the giants in that land of Canaan will be made like bread for them when God makes it possible for them to tread on their land and advised them not to fear. They repeated that the defense of the giants is gone and the LORD was with Israel.

In spite of all the assurances from Joshua and Caleb and Moses and Aaron falling in obeisance to them requesting them to pay heed to the LORD and them, the congregation stoned them. It was at this time that the glory of the LORD appeared in the tabernacle of the congregation before all the children of Israel. The LORD spoke and said to Moses of His disapproval of the cry of the children of Israel. The LORD asked how long these people kept on provoking Him and how long would it take before they fully trusted the LORD. The LORD showed signs and miracles among them, yet they rebelled against Him. The LORD was very angry on the children of Israel and said that He will smite them with pestilence and disinherit them.

The consequence of their disobedience was very serious. All those who were above the age of twenty years including Moses and Aaron, who disobeyed God at some point in their life, did not have the privilege of seeing the Promised Land.

Later, Joshua led the rest of them into the land of Canaan and demanded a promise from the people that they will put away strange gods from among them and serve the LORD. Then, all the people said to Joshua saying that they chose the LORD to serve him.

"And the people said unto Joshua, The LORD our God will we serve, and his voice will we obey". (Joshua 24:24)

Believe in the Lord and he will supply all your needs according to His riches in glory by Christ Jesus.

But my God shall supply all your need according to his riches in glory by Christ Jesus. (Philippians 4:19)

CHAPTER 24
COMFORT IN GOD

"I will both lay me down in peace, and sleep: for thou, LORD, only makest me dwell in safety" Psalm 4:8

King David's life is filled with experiences worth noting, and they are very useful for our exhortation, glorying God in our lives, and for reproof, where necessary. Although he committed serious sins in his life, yet because he confessed his sins to God, he was forgiven, and God called him a man after His own heart not because God approved David's sin, but because he pursued God's ways.

King Saul pursued after his own heart, while David went after the heart of God. Even though God rejected Saul, he did not reject His own people, Israel. And, David was the right choice to be the king over Israel, according to God. The LORD raised a king over Israel, a man whose heart was as compassionate as His, was. God loved Israel and the children of Israel.

"And when he had removed him, he raised up unto them David to be their king; to whom also he gave testimony, and said, I have found David the [son] of Jesse, a man after mine own heart, which shall fulfil all my will" Acts 13:22

David's turmoil, troubles, loss of peace of mind on certain occasions, trials were all within the permissive limits of God. Some of the facts of his life are, as God said, the sword shall never depart from his house; he shall not build a house for the Lord, but his desire shall be fulfilled by his son, Solomon.

The occasion when Psalm 4 was written by David is not revealed in the Scriptures. However, David's acknowledgment of God's help in times of need, and his cry over his enemies and his comfort in the LORD, are clearly evident. His prayer was so passionate and intense that God could not have gone without answering him.

David addresses God, in Psalm 4:1, as God of righteousness, thus acknowledging God's love and mercy towards him. He gave pre-eminence to God in his prayer, and depended on Him, before he ventured on any serious task.

David acknowledged that God enlarged him when he was in distress. He sought God's mercy upon him. His acknowledgment of God's help recalls his victory over philistine giant, Goliath, and in many battles. He was known as 'man of wars', and rightly so, he was triumphant in all, but one battle, where he counted the number of men his army. God said to him to rely fully on Him, but on one occasion, he counted his own strength, and when he tried to depend on his own strength he failed.

When we depend on God we are sure of gaining victory because God is mighty; but when we depend on our strength, we often face defeats, because our strength is limited, and may not be as mighty as of the enemy is. Therefore, it is essential that we always seek God's help, and depend on His strength, because His strength never fails. He delivered the children of Israel with His mighty and outstretched arm; and He is available for us too, for delivering us from our stressful, disastrous and trying situations.

David saw in his life, people, who turned his glory into shame, and, therefore, he questioned them as to how long they would try to bring shame to him. He questioned them if they wished to continue to love vanity. He wanted them to know that the LORD has set apart His people, for Himself, and says that he being one such man, who was set apart for God, the LORD will hear them when he calls unto Him in prayer.

Therefore, David admonishes those who try to bring shame to him, to stand in awe of God and not sin; but introspect themselves when they are on their beds, and be calm. He advises them to offer sacrifices of righteousness, and trust in the LORD.

Many would say to him as to who would do any good to them, but David trusts in the LORD and seeks His help on behalf all of them. He acknowledges that God has put gladness in his heart, more when he was in distress, rather than in situations of abundance, and plenteous of material possessions.

Then, he consoles himself and lays down to sleep in peace because he was sure that he will abide in the LORD's safety.

People, during the time when Lord Jesus Christ was on this earth, tried to bring shame to His glorious works, yet He bore our sins on Him. He died for our sake on the cross bearing our sin to redeem us from our sin. He was buried, and was raised on the third day. Whosoever believes that He is the Lord and believes in his heart that God raised Him from the dead will receive everlasting life. (cf.. 2 Corinthians 5:21, Romans 10:9, John 3:16)

CHAPTER 25
PILLARS IN HEAVEN

Pillars are the strength of monuments and on the pillars are seen inscriptions or designs that either brings to us some remembrance of those, who responsibly raised them, or help us, admire their beauty.

Heaven does not need any pillar to support it, but the New Jerusalem that John saw in his vision coming down from heaven was like a bride adorned for her bridegroom. In this New Jerusalem were seen the pillars on which were written the names of those, who served the living God and the name of the God whom they served.

Some in the Church at Philadelphia had not defiled their garments and they were worthy to receive blessings. God promised that he who overcomes shall walk with Him (Rev 3:3-5).

This is the difference between the earthly Jerusalem and the New Jerusalem that comes down from heaven. John saw a new heaven and a new earth after the first heaven and the first earth passed away and there was no more sea.

In this New Jerusalem there was not seen any difference between Jews or Gentiles, but those who were there were all one in Christ. They had put on righteousness of Christ as their garments. They had received Jesus as their personal Savior and Lord by grace through faith in him.

More than anyone taking airs of his belonging to any clan the important fact that is to be borne in mind is that it is the grace of God that saves a man.

No man needs precious metals such as gold or silver to earn a place in new Jerusalem, but all that a man needs is to have simple faith in Jesus, the Son of God and make him Lord of his/her life. God wipes away their tears.

There shall be no more death, no more sorrow, and no more crying and no more pain. God shall give freely to all that thirst for such a life the fountain of life. He who overcomes the world and the temptations therein shall inherit the blessings from God and he shall be His son. (Rev. 21:2-7)

CHAPTER 26
JERUSALEM AND ITS NEW NAME

The Holy city Jerusalem, the city of our Lord, is now desolate and not in good shape. The city is forsaken and destroyed. But, the day will come when the city will be called "Hephzibah", and its land "Beulah". The Lord delights in making the city delightful for everyone and the land like married woman. (Isaiah Ch. 62:4). This is a prophecy about the status of Jerusalem in the millennial kingdom of Jesus.

Lord Jesus Christ is the Messiah. The Jews rejected him and called upon them the blood of Jesus in order that he may be crucified (Matthew 27:24-25). Peter's speech testifies about those who crucified Jesus.

"Ye men of Israel, hear these words; Jesus of Nazareth, a man approved of God among you by miracles and wonders and signs, which God did by him in the midst of you, as ye yourselves also know: Him, being delivered by the determinate counsel and foreknowledge of God, ye have taken, and by wicked hands have crucified and slain" (Acts 2:22-23)

Indeed, they paid the price in AD 70 according to historians. Earlier, they worshipped idols many-a-time and were chastised by God. They rebelled against God and paid the price for their actions. Yet, they are his people; the city of David is his city.

Like Boaz, who was kinsman redeemer of Ruth, Jesus is our redeemer. He came into this world, died for our sins, was buried, rose from the dead on the third day and later ascended into heaven. He is seated on the right hand of the Majesty and interceding for us.

We, who are redeemed by the blood of Christ, are greater than the unrepentant Jews. But for those, who have accepted Jesus as their personal savior, there is no condemnation irrespective of their race, ethnicity, color, or creed.

Lord Jesus, who is the messiah, speaks and says that he will not sit quite, nor will he rest until he redeems city of Jerusalem again. He defeats the kings loyal to Antichrist at "Armageddon", and sits on the throne of David and literally rules. In the thousand years of his rule there shall be perfect peace.

Satan will be bound with chains and thrown into abyss by an angel who comes from heaven. Later Satan will be released for a short time when he goes Gog and Magog to deceive the nations but fire from God comes down from heaven and devours Satan. (Revelation Ch. 20:8) The dead who did not accept Jesus Christ as their personal savior will resurrect at that time.

The Lord shall judge them at the 'Great white throne' and cast them along with death, hell, and the devil and his angels into the 'lake of fire' to be tormented for ever and ever. This is the second death. For those who are saved, there is no second death but they will have everlasting life to be with the Lord for ever and ever. Note here when Antichrist and false prophet are thrown into the lake of fire! It is before the devil that deceived!!!

Revelation 20:10 confirms it. When the devil was cast into the lake of fire, the Antichrist and the false prophet were already there in the lake of fire.

These are only the ones who will be in the lake of fire before the 'Great White Throne Judgment' (Revelation 16:16 and Revelation 20:8-10). Do Scriptures say that anybody was thrown into the lake of fire or will be thrown into lake of fire before Antichrist and false prophet? No! They are the first one to be thrown into lake of fire.

There shall come out of heaven a New Jerusalem and we, who are saved, shall be in that Holy City. The Church is the bride of our Lord Jesus Christ.

Lord Jesus says that he has set watchmen upon the walls of Jerusalem and they will not keep quite nor will sleep but keep a watch over the city and will make the city a praise of the earth.

This is a promise of Messiah and he has sworn by his right hand and by the arm of his strength. Messiah promised that no more the enemies of Jerusalem will eat its corn as their food no stranger will ever drink its wine. Gentiles will see its righteousness and kings will glory.

"And the Gentiles shall see thy righteousness, and all kings thy glory: and thou shalt be called by a new name, which the mouth of the LORD shall name." (Isaiah 62:2)

THE CHURCH AND THE KINGDOM

----

www.ingramcontent.com/pod-product-compliance
Lightning Source LLC
Chambersburg PA
CBHW060509030426
42337CB00015B/1809